Aerial Ballet The Art and Science Of Flight Adaptations

By
Ehsan Sheroy

INDEX Page Nos

INTRODUCTION

In the immense woven artwork of the normal world, not many peculiarities catch the creative mind and interest of people as significantly as flight. Whether saw in the easy skim of a taking off bird, the complex dance of a butterfly, or the quiet, nighttime quests for a bat, flight is a scene that rises above the limits of the earthbound domain. It is an ensemble of development and transformation — an ethereal artful dance that unfurls across the skies, exhibiting the mind boggling transaction of creativity and logical accuracy.

The peculiarity of flight isn't bound to a solitary scientific classification; a demonstration of the different systems have developed across the tree of life. From the sensitive vacillating of bugs to the great breadth of avian wings and the controlled trapeze artistry of bats, each flying living being has sharpened its interesting procedure, formed by a long period of time of transformative calibrating. However, in the midst of this variety, there are hidden rules that join the craftsmanship and study of flight variations.

This investigation into the universe of flying expressive dance is an encouragement to dive into the wonders of flight — both the stunning movement saw in the normal world and the logical rules that support this apparently mystical capacity. In "Flying Expressive dance: The Workmanship and Study of Flight Variations," we leave on an excursion that navigates the domains of science, physical science, and designing, disentangling the secrets of trip from the perspective of development and advancement.

Section One: Wings of Miracle

Our process starts with an investigation of the designs that make flight conceivable. Wings, in their heap structures, act as the material whereupon the expressive dance of the skies Is painted. From the prolonged wings of taking off birds to the mind boggling plans of bug wings, we dive into the life structures that empowers lift, drag, and the agile moving fundamental for endurance. The physical science of flight turns into a convincing story, told from the perspective of wing morphology and its exceptional variations.

Experts of the Sky

Birds, the undisputed experts of the sky, become the overwhelming focus in this section. Avian greatness is uncovered through the assorted flying strategies utilized by various species. Through a similar examination, we uncover the subtleties of trip in birds, investigating their actual transformations as well as the social procedures that add to their ethereal ability. It is a festival of the padded specialists whose exhibitions elegance our skies.

Past Plumes - Bug Flying

The ethereal artful dance reaches out past birds to the smaller than usual virtuosos of the bug world. In this section, we direct our concentration toward the striking variations that empower bugs to explore the air with unmatched readiness. The complexities of wing shape, size, and the quick beat of sensitive wings become the point of convergence as we disentangle the insider facts of bug flight. Furthermore, we dive into the developmental weapons contest among bugs and their hunters, an artful dance of endurance that has formed the bug world.

Flying Warm blooded animals - Bats At the center of attention

Bats, the main well evolved creatures fit for supported flight, become the overwhelming focus in this part. As nighttime pilots, bats have advanced special variations in life systems and physiology. Echolocation turns into a vital component in their flying artful dance, permitting them to explore the haziness with shocking accuracy. Past their cryptic flight, we investigate the environmental significance of bats as pollinators and regulators of bug populaces, featuring the interconnectedness of species in the fragile dance of biological systems.

People Take Off

Mankind's journey for flight has been a demonstration of development and designing ability. In this part, we follow the set of experiences and advancement of human flight — from the early fantasies about taking off like birds to the mechanical wonders that characterize present day avionics. The crossing point of workmanship and science becomes obvious as we investigate the social and imaginative effect of human-made flight, changing the skies into a material for both mechanical accomplishment and inventive articulation.

The Artful dance of Movement

Relocation, a peculiarity imbued in the texture of many flying species, becomes the dominant focal point in this section. We investigate the spectacular excursions of transitory creatures, uncovering the complicated navigational abilities and transformations that empower them to cross immense distances. The expressive dance of movement turns into an account of endurance, biological equilibrium, and the difficulties presented by an influencing world. Preservation endeavors arise as a vital topic as we mull over the sensitive movement of relocation notwithstanding natural dangers.

Trip from here on out
Our process finishes up by looking into the fate of flight. We look at the continuous developments in flying and the blossoming field of biomimicry, where human designing looks for motivation from the regular world. Moral contemplations and the natural effect of arising flight advances become the overwhelming focus as we explore the sensitive harmony among progress and environmental obligation. The end section considers the immortal journey to unwind the secrets of elevated expressive dance and the likely effect of our undertakings on the fragile movement of the skies.

This investigation into the craftsmanship and study of flight variations is a tribute to the excellence intrinsic in the airborne expressive dance that unfurls above and around us. Through fastidious exploration, spellbinding stories, and a blend of different logical disciplines, "Elevated Expressive dance" looks to rouse miracle and appreciation for the many-sided embroidery of trip in the regular world. Go along with us as we lift off into the endless span of the skies, where masterfulness and science combine in an entrancing dance of variation and development.

A.   Definition and significance of flight adaptations

Flight, an apparently ethereal capacity held for the avian world, bugs, and bats, has enamored the human creative mind since days of yore. The thought of challenging gravity, of taking off through the skies, has started dreams, folklores, and mechanical headways. In the mind boggling embroidery of the normal world, flight variations arise as a demonstration of the clever manners by which life forms have developed to vanquish the difficulties presented by the three-layered domain. This investigation digs into the definition and meaning of flight transformations, disentangling the intricacies of how different species have become amazing at getting off the ground.

Characterizing Flight Variations: The Developmental Ensemble
At its center, flight variation alludes to the set-up of physical, physiological, and social alterations that empower an organic entity to travel through the air with proficiency and control. These variations are the consequence of a multifaceted dance among development and normal choice, an orchestra of hereditary changes finely tuned to the requests of flying life.

Life systems of Flight: Wings, Appendages, and Then some
The most notorious sign of flight variations is, without a doubt, the improvement of wings. Wings come in different structures, each custom fitted to the particular necessities of the living being. Birds brag padded wings that give both lift and exact control during flight.

Bugs, then again, feature a different cluster of wing structures, from the fragile membranous wings of butterflies to the strong exoskeletal wings of creepy crawlies. Bats, the main well evolved creatures fit for supported flight, take care of stretched fingers in a flimsy film, shaping their wing structure.

Past wings, other physical variations assume a pivotal part. Lightweight skeletons decrease by and large weight, working with lift. Strong frameworks are finely tuned to oblige the energy requests of supported flight. The respiratory framework advances to productively extricate oxygen from the air, supporting the high metabolic rates expected for aeronautical undertakings.

Physiological Authority: Energy and Digestion

Flight is a vivaciously requesting try, requiring a dominance of metabolic cycles. Creatures adjusted for flight have developed effective approaches to removing energy from their environmental elements. For example, birds have exceptionally productive respiratory frameworks, highlighting air sacs that take into consideration a ceaseless progression of oxygen, guaranteeing a steady stock during both inward breath and exhalation. This transformation boosts oxygen trade, a basic figure supporting the high metabolic rates related with flight.

Also, variations in the cardiovascular framework are foremost. Birds, for example, have hearts relatively bigger than those of non-flying creatures, siphoning oxygenated blood to the muscles at a sped up rate during flight. This physiological coordination guarantees that the energy requests of flight are met with accuracy.

Conduct Movement: Route and Correspondence

Flight transformations reach out past life structures and physiology to include unpredictable social procedures. Route is an essential viewpoint, particularly for transient species. Birds, eminent for their transient accomplishments, frequently show momentous navigational capacities, depending on divine signals, milestones, and, surprisingly, Earth's attractive field for direction. Bugs, as well, exhibit multifaceted navigational ways of behaving, for certain species setting out on legendary excursions across mainlands.

Correspondence in the air adds one more layer to the artful dance of flight. Vocalizations, visual shows, and, surprisingly, synchronized developments become significant for species took part in ethereal romance or gathering ways of behaving. The meaning of such conduct transformations lies in their job in individual endurance as well as in the more extensive setting of species propagation and environmental equilibrium.

The Meaning of Flight Transformations: Unwinding Nature's Airborne Embroidered artwork

Endurance and Predation: The Sky as a War zone

In the developmental weapons contest, flight transformations are both protective layer and weapon. The capacity to take to the skies offers an unmistakable benefit in dodging hunters or seeking after prey. Flying predators, like birds and hawks, feature unmatched ethereal ability in hunting, utilizing sharp vision and exact moving to get their feasts. On the other hand, prey species frequently foster shifty flying moves or mimicry to get away from the grip of airborne hunters.

The meaning of these variations stretches out past simple endurance; it shapes environments by affecting hunter prey elements, populace sizes, and, surprisingly, the conveyance of species inside living spaces.

Asset Procurement and Abuse: Exploring the Air for Food

Flight variations open new roads for asset securing. Birds, with their capacity to cover huge distances, can take advantage of occasional food sources, be it relocating to hotter environments or following the blooming of explicit plants. Bugs, as pollinators, assume a crucial part in the multiplication of various plant species, shaping complicated natural organizations.

The importance lies in individual scavenging systems as well as in the more extensive environmental associations fashioned through aeronautical connections. The development of pollinators, for instance, works with the variety and versatility of biological systems by supporting plant generation.

Natural Availability: The Skyways of Life

The meaning of flight transformations resonates through natural network. Relocation, a peculiarity imbued in the existence chronicles of numerous species, fills in as an essential string interfacing far off living spaces. Birds, bugs, and, surprisingly, a few warm blooded creatures navigate landmasses, connecting environments and working with the trading of hereditary material, supplements, and even microorganisms.

As environmental change and natural surroundings discontinuity reshape scenes, the capacity to cross these changed conditions turns out to be progressively critical. Flight variations, consequently, add to the versatility of species and biological systems notwithstanding natural difficulties.

Social and Tasteful Worth: Moving Human Creative mind

Flight variations hold an exceptional spot in human culture and style. Birds, with their elegant flights and melodic tunes, have propelled workmanship, writing, and folklore all through mankind's set of experiences.

Bugs, with their energetic varieties and sensitive moves, add to the stylish lavishness of regular scenes. The ethereal scene of bats in flight, outlined against the sundown sky, has ignited interest and strange notion.

The importance here lies in the natural worth of flight variations past their biological jobs. They act as a wellspring of motivation, cultivating a profound association among people and the normal world.

B. Evolutionary perspective on the development of flight in various species

Flight, a zenith of biomechanical accomplishment, has freely developed in different heredities across the tree of life. From the taking off greatness of birds to the fragile shudder of butterflies and the nighttime tumbling of bats, the development of flight is a dazzling story that unfurls north of millions of years. This investigation digs into the transformative points of view on the advancement of trip in various species, disentangling the extraordinary pathways that have prompted aeronautical dominance.

1. The Beginning of Flight: Bugs Get off the ground

The transformative beginnings of flight track down their underlying foundations in the old world, with bugs arising as trailblazers in the ethereal domain. The earliest bugs, roughly quite a while back, explored a world overwhelmed by transcending plants and coming up short on complex wings found in their cutting edge partners. Through a course of normal determination, those with limbs that took into consideration controlled coasting or short flights acquired an unmistakable benefit. Over ages, these simple wings advanced into the assorted exhibit of wing structures saw in the present bugs. The improvement of trip in bugs is a demonstration of the versatile force of steady changes. As wings turned out to be more particular for different biological specialties, bugs broadened into a horde of structures — from the spry dragonflies that watch water bodies to the fragile butterflies that effortlessness glades. The development of trip in bugs exhibits the flexibility of this variation and its job in taking advantage of different territories and assets.

2. Avian Tastefulness: The Dominance of Padded Flight

The development of trip in birds is a story of refinement and flawlessness. While the specific starting points of avian flight stay a subject of logical request, the change from ground-staying dinosaurs to padded, flying birds is a legitimate interaction. Feathers, at first advanced for protection and show, bit by bit adjusted for streamlined purposes. The Archaeopteryx, a renowned temporary fossil from the Late Jurassic time frame, offers a brief look into this developmental excursion. With padded wings and a skeletal design demonstrative of flight capacity, the Archaeopteryx addresses a transitional stage between non-avian dinosaurs and current birds.

Resulting transformative advancements, like the improvement of a fall for muscle connection, empty bones for diminished weight, and a profoundly proficient respiratory framework, impelled birds into the skies with unrivaled dominance.

The versatile radiation of birds prompted a different cluster of flying methodologies, from the taking off beauty of hawks to the nimble moving of hummingbirds. Flight, in the avian genealogy, became a method for movement as well as a foundation of their environmental achievement, permitting them to take advantage of fluctuated natural surroundings, access assets, and stay away from predation.

3. Bats: The Mammalian Pilots

Bats, the main warm blooded creatures fit for supported flight, address a special part in the developmental adventure of elevated dominance. The development of trip in bats is complicatedly attached to the versatile tensions of their nighttime way of life and dietary inclinations. The earliest bats, showing up around quite a while back, possible had coasting capacities that bit by bit developed into fueled flight.

A vital element of bat flight is the prolongation of the fingers, which support the wing layer. This physical variation, alongside an exceptionally adaptable skeleton, permits bats to execute complex flying moves. Echolocation, an organic sonar framework developed freely by bats, further improves their capacity to explore and catch prey in obscurity.

The transformative progress of bats as nighttime fliers is apparent in their worldwide circulation and various natural jobs. From organic product bats distributing seeds in tropical woodlands to bug eating bats giving regular nuisance control, the developmental direction of trip in bats is firmly entwined with their natural commitments.

4. Pterosaurs: The Rulers of the Mesozoic Skies

In the Mesozoic Period, a gathering of reptiles known as pterosaurs took off through the skies, possessing a specialty like that of present day birds. Pterosaurs advanced autonomously of birds and bats, displaying focalized development in the improvement of flight variations. These antiquated flyers, with their rugged wings and different sizes, filled environmental jobs going from fish-hunting beach front occupants to taking off dominant hunters.

The advancement of trip in pterosaurs features the versatility of flight designs to various natural specialties. Their wings, upheld by a stretched fourth finger, bore similitudes to bat wings, yet the construction of their other skeletons varied essentially. The capacity to get off the ground permitted pterosaurs to take advantage of different territories, from marine conditions to inland scenes.

The elimination of pterosaurs toward the finish of the Cretaceous time frame denoted the conclusion of an important time period, making ready for the ascent of present day birds as the prevailing aeronautical vertebrates. By the by, the developmental history of pterosaurs fills in as an entrancing part in the more extensive story of flight variation.

5. Human Climb: A Mechanical Development

The development of flight isn't restricted to the domain of science; people, with their resourcefulness and mechanical ability, have set out on their own excursion into the skies. While our far off progenitors could merely fantasize about taking off like birds, the development of human flight is an account of designing, development, and steadiness. The earliest endeavors at flight, frequently propelled by perceptions of birds, were set apart by experimentation. The fantasy of human flight turned into a reality in the mid twentieth hundred years with the coming of fueled, controlled flight. The Wright siblings, Orville and Wilbur, accomplished the main supported, controlled trip in 1903, everlastingly adjusting the direction of mankind's set of experiences.

The resulting development of aeronautics saw quick headways, from the advancement of business air travel to space investigation. Human flight, when a far off dream, has turned into a basic piece of current life, molding worldwide network, trade, and social trade.

6. Developmental Weapons contest and Coevolution: The Dance of Hunters and Prey

The development of trip in different species isn't simply a single excursion yet a unique dance formed by the connections among hunters and prey. The skies become a front line where variations for pursuit and avoidance unfurl in an unending weapons contest. Flying predators, with their sharp visual perception and strong claws, take part in elevated pursuits that require both accuracy and speed. Accordingly, prey species foster shifty moves, for example, whimsical flight examples or disguise, to get away from their airborne hunters.

Likewise, the advancement of bug flight is laced with the systems of their hunters. Insectivorous birds and bats, furnished with specific variations for elevated hunting, apply particular tensions that shape the development of bug flight capacities. The dance among hunters and prey in the flying domain highlights the interconnectedness of species and the job of trip in molding biological elements.

C. Overview of the book's exploration of the art and science of aerial ballet

In the pages of "Flying Expressive dance: The Craftsmanship and Study of Flight Transformations," perusers are welcome to leave on a charming excursion through the vast skies, investigating the many-sided transaction of masterfulness and logical accuracy that characterizes the universe of flight variations. This far reaching outline gives a brief look into the different sections that unfurl inside the book, winding around together the magnificence of nature's elevated expressive dance and the basic rules that oversee the flight transformations of different species.

1. Revealing the Privileged insights of Winged Miracles: Part One

The excursion begins with a profound plunge into the life systems and mechanics of trip in "Wings of Marvel." Here, the spotlight is on the wings — the exquisite designs that characterize the flying artful dance of birds, bugs, and bats. Perusers are taken on a visit through the material science of flight, from lift and drag to the subtleties of wing morphology. The section fills in as an establishment, exposing the fundamental components that set up for the striking exhibitions of animals taking off.

Through enrapturing accounts and definite outlines, perusers gain a comprehension of how the developmental weapons contest has formed the assorted variations seen in winged organic entities. From the stretched wings of taking off birds to the sensitive wing-beats of bugs and the layer covered wings of bats, every variation is a magnum opus etched by the powers of normal choice.

2. Avian Greatness: The Artful dance of Padded Virtuosos - Section Two

The subsequent section, "Experts of the Sky," moves the concentration to the avian domain, where birds become the dominant focal point in the airborne expressive dance. Here, perusers dig into the universe of avian greatness, investigating the fluctuated flying strategies utilized by various bird species. Through a relative examination, the section discloses the subtleties of trip in birds — featuring the transformations that recognize ethereal trackers, transitory wonders, and nimble foragers.

Social variations, from romance presentations to unpredictable group developments, are investigated, portraying the variety inside the avian artful dance. Perusers witness the association between life systems, conduct, and environmental jobs as birds effortlessly explore the three-layered material of the sky.

3. Past Quills - Bug Aviation: Section Three

The third part, "Past Plumes - Bug Air transportation," brings perusers into the small scale universe of bugs, where flight is an orchestra of fragile moves. From the drifting trip of hummingbirds to the unpredictable moves of butterflies, this section unwinds the privileged insights of bug flight instruments.

Wing shape, size, and the fast beat of wings become central focuses in understanding how bugs explore the air with unmatched nimbleness.

The transformative variations of bugs in the weapons contest against hunters and contenders are disclosed, displaying the mind boggling variety and creativity present in this modest yet crucial domain of flight. As perusers venture through the pages, they gain a recently discovered appreciation for the biological jobs played by bugs in fertilization, seed dispersal, and the more extensive elements of environments.

4. Flying Warm blooded creatures - Bats At the center of attention: Part Four

Section four, named "Flying Vertebrates - Bats At the center of attention," directs concentration toward the main warm blooded creatures equipped for supported flight. Bats, with their nighttime interests and unpredictable echolocation frameworks, become the dominant focal point in this piece of the airborne expressive dance. Perusers investigate the life systems and physiology that empower bats to explore the dimness with unmatched accuracy.

Past their mysterious flight, the natural significance of bats is highlighted, from their job as pollinators to their commitment in controlling bug populaces. The section winds around together the logical complexities of bat trip with the natural meaning of these nighttime pilots, offering an all encompassing point of view on the expressive dance of flying warm blooded creatures.

5. People Take Off: Section Five

In the fifth section, "People Take Off," the story movements to the human journey for flight. This piece of the excursion follows the authentic and mechanical development of human-made flight, from the early fantasies about taking off like birds to the cutting edge wonders of aeronautics. Perusers witness the crossing point of craftsmanship and science as people break the gravitational limits and take to the skies.

The section digs into the social and imaginative effect of human flight, investigating how flying has changed transportation as well as propelled inventiveness, development, and a feeling of limitless conceivable outcomes. From the Wright siblings' noteworthy trip to the time of business air travel and space investigation, the human section in the flying expressive dance unfurls with dazzling stories of accomplishment.

6. The Artful dance of Movement: Section Six

Section six, named "The Artful dance of Movement," turns the focus on one of the most charming parts of flight — the peculiarity of relocation. Here, perusers are taken on a worldwide excursion, investigating the examples and transformations that describe the significant distance trips of different species. From birds crossing mainlands to butterflies leaving on legendary excursions, the part disentangles the secrets of route, natural prompts, and the biological meaning of movement.

Protection difficulties and arrangements come into center as the section mulls over the sensitive movement of relocation notwithstanding natural changes. The expressive dance of movement turns into an impactful impression of the interconnectedness of species and the requirement for worldwide endeavors to safeguard these striking excursions.

7. Trip from now on: Section Seven

The last section, "Trip from now on," pushes perusers into the domain of mechanical developments and arising flight variations. Here, the book investigates the state of the art advancements in flying and biomimicry, where human designing looks for motivation from the normal world. Moral contemplations and the ecological effect of arising flight advancements are examined as perusers wrestle with the developing crossing point of human-made flight and the sensitive movement of the regular world.

As perusers explore the eventual fate of flight, they are provoked to contemplate the possible results of our innovative interests and the obligation that accompanies imitating the aeronautical transformations culminated by innumerable species through centuries.

Chapter 1
Wings of Wonder

In the tremendous and dynamic venue of the regular world, not many peculiarities bring out a feeling of marvel and esteem as much as the dominance of flight. "Wings of Marvel" digs into the core of this captivating exhibition, investigating the complexities of flight variations that have developed across different species. From the sensitive ripple of butterflies to the taking off greatness of birds and the nighttime gymnastics of bats, the development of wings remains as a demonstration of nature's resourcefulness. This broad investigation discloses the mysteries implanted in the life structures, mechanics, and transformative meaning of wings, uncovering the wonders that unfurl in the skies.

1. The Life structures of Flight:
The excursion into the universe of wings starts with an investigation of their life systems — the fragile yet strong designs that make flight conceivable. Across the range of flying creatures, wings display a wonderful variety formed by developmental tensions and natural specialties.

Bird Wings:
The tastefulness of bird wings, with their complex quill structures, becomes the dominant focal point. Each plume fills a need, from giving lift and mobility to supporting thermoregulation and show. The progressive plan of plumes and the presence of specific elements like alulae add to the streamlined proficiency that characterizes avian flight.
The fluctuating states of wings among various bird species mirror their biological jobs. Taking off raptors have expansive wings for effective coasting, while spry larks brag pointed wings appropriate for speedy and exact moves. This variety in wing morphology is a demonstration of the flexibility of flight designs to the requests of explicit conditions.

Bug Wings:
Progressing to the small universe of bugs, the intricacy of bug wings unfurls. Dissimilar to the plumes of birds, bug wings are membranous, upheld by an organization of veins. This section takes apart the multifaceted varieties in wing shape and construction, displaying variations that reach from the complex rear wings of scarabs to the sensitive wings of butterflies.
The adaptability of bug wings stretches out to their capability past flight. Wings can act as thermoregulatory organs, sound-creating designs, or safeguards for protection.

The transformative developments in the bug domain highlight the assorted environmental jobs played by these entrancing creatures.

Bat Wings:
The investigation of wings extends to the main warm blooded creatures equipped for supported flight — bats. The life systems of bat wings is a wonder of development, with stretched fingers supporting a slim layer that shapes the wing structure. This section digs into the transformations that empower bats to execute perplexing airborne moves, from quick goes to floating.

The uniqueness of bat wings reaches out to their adaptability in different biological specialties. A few bats are adjusted for accuracy in catching bugs, while others have long, tight wings for effective significant distance flights. The transformative way of bat wings uncovers a unique interaction among structure and capability.

2. The Material science of Flight:
With a primary comprehension of wing life structures, the investigation go on into the material science of flight — the essential rules that oversee the elements of remaining overhead.

Lift and Drag:
Fundamental to the material science of flight are the contradicting powers of lift and drag. This segment clarifies how wings create lift, the power that checks gravity and permits an organic entity to rise. The unpredictable connection between wing shape, airfoil plan, and the approach turns into a point of convergence, underlining the accuracy with which creatures have developed to control these variables. Simultaneously, the job of drag — the opposition experienced as a life form travels through the air — is investigated. Systems for limiting drag, for example, smoothed out wing shapes and wing stacking variations, uncover the streamlining that happens in the transformative journey for proficient flight.

Wing Morphology and Flight Procedures:
The section then, at that point, dives into the association between wing morphology and flight systems. The particular manners by which birds, bugs, and bats convey their wings for different methods of flight — from drifting and skimming to taking off and floating — are complicatedly attached to their environmental jobs and developmental narratives.

Flying predators grandstand taking off procedures, taking advantage of rising air flows for energy proficiency, while hummingbirds display fast, floating flight empowered by specific wing morphology.

he transformative developments in wing configuration line up with the particular requests of an animal varieties' way of life, representing the coevolution of structure and capability.

3. Contextual analyses on Special Wing Transformations:

This portion investigates explicit contextual analyses that feature the extraordinary wing transformations saw in different species. Each contextual investigation fills in as a demonstration of the variety of arrangements that have developed in light of the difficulties and valuable open doors introduced by flight.

Gooney birds:

The gooney bird, an expert of significant distance maritime flight, turns into a point of convergence. Their enormous wingspan, combined with one of a kind wing stacking qualities, permits them to cover immense distances with negligible exertion. The transformative benefits of such variations for scavenging over broad maritime regions are investigated, revealing insight into the exceptional navigational capacities of these seabirds.

Moths:

Moving to the domain of nighttime flight, the contextual analysis on moths discloses the interesting difficulties presented by low-light circumstances. The advancement of particular wing designs and examples that upgrade mobility and disguise becomes obvious. The complex transaction between wing transformations and the nighttime biology of moths offers bits of knowledge into the quiet expressive dance of these animals in obscurity.

Dragonflies:

The gymnastic trips of dragonflies become the dominant focal point for this situation study. Their outstanding dexterity, quick speed increases, and exact hunting moves are taken apart with regards to wing morphology. The advancement of specific muscles and control instruments uncovers the many-sided systems that empower dragonflies to explore complex conditions with unrivaled ability.

4. Social Transformations for Elevated Endurance:

Past the actual parts of wings, this segment investigates the social transformations that supplement physical highlights, adding to the general progress of flying endurance.

Romance Showcases:

Ethereal romance showcases arise as an intriguing part of conduct variations. Birds participate in intricate elevated exhibitions, displaying their actual ability as well as their hereditary wellness.

From the bewildering showcases of birds of heaven to the synchronized trips of seeking matches, the section disentangles the association between ethereal artful dance and regenerative achievement.

Relocation Methodologies:
The wonder of relocation turns into a point of convergence, representing how wings are instruments of movement as well as navigational devices. The section looks at the complex systems utilized by transitory species, like the utilization of divine prompts, milestones, and, surprisingly, Earth's attractive field. The job of energy-proficient flight designs and the physiological variations that help extremely long travel highlight the complicated movement of relocation.

Bunch Ways of behaving:
Helpful flight ways of behaving become the overwhelming focus as the section investigates the synchronized trips of groups and arrangements. From the multifaceted elevated ballet performances of starlings to the planned V-arrangements of moving birds, the meaning of collective vibes in both hunter aversion and asset procurement becomes clear. The section dives into the correspondence procedures and versatile benefits that support aggregate ethereal ways of behaving.

5. The Craftsmanship and Study of Wing Hue:
This section disentangles the multifaceted connection between wing tinge and the step by step processes for surviving utilized by different flying organic entities. The union of craftsmanship and science is especially obvious in the visual shows and examples displayed by wings.

Cover and Mimicry:
The part investigates how wing tinge fills in as a device for endurance, permitting creatures to mix flawlessly into their surroundings or copy hurtful species. From the secretive examples of butterflies that look like passes on to the mimicry showed by specific moths to look like harmful partners, the transformative weapons contest among hunters and prey unfurls in a visual ensemble.

Correspondence and Show:
Wing shading takes on an open job, filling in as a visual language in the romance ceremonies and regional presentations of different species. The energetic shades of butterfly wings, the radiance of hummingbird feathers, and the complex examples shown during romance moves become a material for the declaration of hereditary wellness and conceptive ability.

6. The Development of Wings: An Excursion Through Topographical Time:
The investigation of wings rises above the present, diving into the developmental annals of these noteworthy variations. This section fills in as an excursion through land time, following the rise and enhancement of wings across various ages.

Paleozoic Flyers:
The starting points of flight are investigated with regards to Paleozoic flyers — early winged organic entities that wandered into the airborne domain. From the main arthropods that coasted through the Carboniferous skies to the assorted cluster of flying bugs that arose during the Permian, the section divulges the developmental analyses that prepared for the different variations saw in current bugs.

Mesozoic Pilots:
The Mesozoic time saw the ascent of airborne reptiles, exemplified by the pterosaurs. With their rough wings and various sizes, pterosaurs turned into the masters of the Mesozoic skies. The section investigates the natural jobs played by these antiquated flyers and the elements that prompted their inevitable annihilation toward the finish of the Cretaceous.

The Ascent of Birds:
The developmental rising of birds becomes the overwhelming focus, following their ancestry from ground-staying dinosaurs to the different cluster of avian structures seen today. The section dives into momentary fossils, for example, the Archaeopteryx, that give experiences into the progressive development of plumes and wings. The versatile radiation of birds across different territories turns into a demonstration of the flexibility and progress of winged transformations.

7. Human Flight: An Innovative Expressive dance:
The story takes a turn towards human accomplishments in flight, exhibiting the mechanical artful dance that has permitted people to challenge gravity. From the fantasies of old developments to the advanced time of business aeronautics and space investigation, this part investigates the development of human-made flight.

The Wright Siblings and Then some:
The spearheading endeavors of the Wright siblings in accomplishing the primary maintained, controlled trip in 1903 imprint a groundbreaking crossroads throughout the entire existence of human flight. The part follows the resulting progressions in avionics, from the brilliant time of air travel to the mechanical jumps that finished in space investigation. The convergence of designing, development, and human desire turns into a demonstration of the unyielding soul of investigation.

Biomimicry and Future Advancements:
The expressive dance of human flight stretches out past the limits of science, with the investigation of biomimicry — the act of drawing motivation from regular plans. Mechanical advancements motivated by the streamlined features of birds and bugs, from fluttering wing robots to smoothed out airplane plans, exhibit the continuous discourse between human resourcefulness and the developmental flawlessness of wings in the normal world.

8. Trip in the Anthropocene: Difficulties and Protection:
The last section of the book considers the difficulties looked by flying living beings in the Anthropocene — the time set apart by human impact. The fragile expressive dance of flight, unpredictably arranged by development, is currently gone up against by anthropogenic dangers going from living space misfortune to environmental change.

Territory Fracture and Urbanization:
The effect of human exercises on normal territories is analyzed, especially the difficulties presented by environment discontinuity and urbanization. As regular scenes are analyzed and changed, the capacity of flying organic entities to explore and flourish is compromised. The part digs into the ramifications for transitory species, pollinators, and other flying creatures.

Environmental Change and Relocation Examples:
The ramifications of environmental change on the sensitive artful dance of movement become the dominant focal point. Adjustments in temperature, precipitation, and occasional prompts upset the finely tuned timetables of transient species. The part investigates how these progressions resound through biological systems, influencing the actual transients as well as the interconnected trap of species that depend on their developments.

Preservation Procedures:
The story closes with a reflection on preservation methodologies pointed toward protecting the wonders of trip despite anthropogenic difficulties. From living space reclamation drives to worldwide endeavors to battle environmental change, the part underlines the requirement for aggregate activity to guarantee the proceeded with presence of the assorted winged ponders that effortlessness the skies.

1.1   Anatomy of wings in different flying organisms (birds, insects, bats)

The capacity to take flight is a surprising transformation that has freely developed in different gatherings of creatures, each making its one of a kind ethereal ability through the complexities of wing life systems. From the padded wings of birds to the membranous wings of bugs and the stretched fingers of bats supporting their wing films, the life structures of wings is a demonstration of the variety of developmental answers for vanquishing the skies. This investigation digs into the particular qualities of wing life systems in birds, bugs, and bats, unwinding the wonders that empower these animals to explore the three-layered domain of flight.

1. Avian Polish: The Padded Wings of Birds

Birds, the prototype pilots of the animals of the world collectively, display a scope of wing variations that have developed more than huge number of years. The key unit of a bird's wing is the plume — a particular construction that serves different capabilities past simple flight.

Feathers and their Capabilities:

Feathers, made out of keratin, are lightweight yet strong designs that structure the essential structure blocks of avian wings. The essential plumes, arranged at the tips of the wings, are vital for producing lift during flight. The course of action of these essential quills, alongside the auxiliary plumes, adds to the wing's airfoil shape, improving lift and limiting drag.

Furthermore, feathers assume an imperative part in thermoregulation, giving protection against temperature limits. During romance presentations, dynamic and glowing quills become apparatuses of visual correspondence, underlining the double idea of plumes as both functional and decorative variations.

Wing Construction and Adaptability:

The wings of birds comprise of three principal areas: the hand-wing, lower arm, and upper arm. The hand-wing is the area past the wrist joint and supports the essential and optional flight feathers. The lower arm compares to the segment between the wrist and elbow, while the upper arm reaches out from the elbow to the shoulder joint.

The skeletal construction of the wing is described by melded wrist and finger bones, bringing about an unbending yet profoundly flexibility limb. The jointed idea of the wing considers changes in wing shape during flight, adding to the bird's capacity to execute complicated aeronautical moves.

Birds likewise have specific muscles that control wing developments. The pectoralis major, the essential muscle liable for downstroke during flight, is a huge piece of the bird's weight. The supracoracoideus muscle, situated on the fall bone, controls the upstroke, making a finely tuned interchange of muscles for supported flight.

Variations for Various Flight Styles:
The life structures of bird wings shifts as indicated by the species' natural specialty and flight necessities. Taking off birds, similar to hawks and vultures, frequently have long, expansive wings for proficient floating. Interestingly, birds that require quick and light-footed flight, like hummingbirds, have more limited, more pointed wings. This variety in wing morphology mirrors the versatility of birds to take advantage of different natural specialties.

2. Bug Air transportation: The Membranous Wings of Minuscule Wonders
Bugs, with their little size and exceptional variety, have vanquished the skies utilizing something else entirely structure — membranous wings. Not at all like the plumes of birds, bug wings comprise of a slender, straightforward layer upheld by an organization of veins.

Wing Morphology and Enunciation:
The wings of bugs are joined to the chest, with the forewings and hindwings frequently showing varieties in size and shape. The membranous idea of bug wings considers adaptability and empowers an extensive variety of wing developments, including fluttering, skimming, and drifting.
The explanation of bug wings is a particular element that improves their mobility. The capacity to overlap wings firmly against the body when not being used is basic for limiting air obstruction and working with different exercises, like taking care of or mating. In certain species, for example, bugs, the forewings have developed into solidified structures known as elytra, which serve a defensive capability. At the point when the bug is in flight, the elytra are lifted, permitting the membranous hindwings to unfurl and give the vital lift.

Solid Control and Flight Styles:
The control of bug wings depends on a refined arrangement of muscles, which are joined to the chest. The hostile activity of these muscles permits bugs to tweak wing developments quickly. Bugs are equipped for executing complex airborne moves, like quick shifts in course and drifting, because of the exact control managed the cost of by their wing muscular structure.

The variety in bug flight styles is tremendous, going from the maintained and deft trip of honey bees to the sporadic and sly trip of butterflies. The wing morphology and muscle structure are finely tuned to the biological requests of every species, showing the fantastic flexibility of bugs in exploring their surroundings.

3. Bats: Mammalian Pilots with Extended Fingers and Layers

Bats, as the main well evolved creatures fit for supported flight, have a wing structure that is particular from the two birds and bugs. Their wings are shaped by a film extended between lengthened fingers, making an adaptable and productive surface for ethereal moving.

Prolonged Fingers and Wing Film:

The most striking component of bat wings is the extension of the fingers, especially the second to fifth digits. The wing layer, known as the patagium, is extended between these lengthened fingers and reaches out down to the hindlimbs and tail. The adaptability of the patagium permits bats to change wing shape powerfully, acclimating to the requests of various flight moves.

The stretched fingers likewise add to the calibrating of wing developments. By articulating their fingers and changing the pressure in the patagium, bats can execute exact elevated tumbling, from sharp goes to fast jumps.

Muscle Life systems and Flight Control:

The flight muscles of bats are amassed in the chest and back, with the pectoralis muscles liable for the downstroke and the supracoracoideus muscles fueling the upstroke. The power created by these muscles, joined with the adaptability of the wing structure, permits bats to accomplish noteworthy deftness in flight.

Bats additionally have specific muscles in the wing film, permitting them to adjust the camber and ebb and flow of the wing during flight. This versatility is essential for exploring through jumbled conditions, like thick vegetation, where accuracy in flight is vital.

Echolocation and Flight Proficiency:

Bats have developed a refined echolocation framework, further improving their flight capacities. By transmitting high-recurrence sound waves and breaking down the returning reverberations, bats can explore, find prey, and stay away from deterrents in complete haziness. Echolocation supplements the proficiency of their flight, permitting bats to take advantage of nighttime biological specialties.

The mix of stretched fingers, membranous wings, and echolocation has moved bats into different environmental jobs, from insectivorous trackers to nectar feeders and natural product eaters. Their physical variations highlight the flexibility of flight structures in fulfilling the assorted needs of various ways of life.

1.2   The physics of flight: lift, drag, and the role of wing morphology

Flight, the specialty of opposing gravity and exploring the skies, is a complicated transaction of actual powers and physical transformations. The major standards administering flight — lift and drag — are complicatedly connected to the morphology of wings, which change fundamentally among flying creatures. From the taking off wings of falcons to the fragile layers of bats and the multifaceted venation of bug wings, every transformation is finely tuned to upgrade execution in unambiguous natural specialties. This investigation digs into the physical science of flight, unwinding the components behind lift and drag, and looking at how wing morphology assumes a significant part in the dominance of the elevated domain.

1. Lift: Resisting Gravity with Streamlined Accuracy

Lift Age:

At the core of flight is the age of lift, the power that goes against gravity and permits creatures to climb up high. Lift is made by taking advantage of the standards of optimal design, especially the association between the wing and the air it travels through.
The state of the wing assumes an essential part in lift age. A typical confusion is that lift is exclusively a consequence of wind current over the bended upper surface of the wing, making lower pressure and lifting the organic entity. As a general rule, lift is an outcome of the strain distinction between the upper and lower surfaces of the wing, which is principally impacted by the wing's approach and airfoil plan.

Approach:

The approach is the point between the harmony line of the wing (a fanciful straight line from the main edge to the following edge) and the approaching air. By changing the approach, organic entities have some control over the lift created by their wings. Notwithstanding, there is an ideal approach for most extreme lift, past which wind stream becomes fierce, causing a slow down — an unexpected and uncontrolled loss of lift.
Birds, bugs, and bats have advanced various techniques to deal with their approach. Birds, for example, can adjust the state of their wings during trip to streamline lift and lessen drag. Bugs, with their membranous wings, can misshape their wing construction to powerfully change the approach. Bats, with their adaptable wing layers, can change the shape of their wings to accomplish the ideal lift.

Airfoil Plan:
The airfoil plan of the wing — a cross-sectional shape that boosts lift and limits drag —
is a basic calculate lift age. An ordinary airfoil has a bended upper surface and a
compliment lower surface. As wind currents over the wing, the bended upper surface
outcomes in quicker wind stream, making lower strain as per Bernoulli's guideline. In the
mean time, the compliment lower surface keeps up with higher tension, creating a
vertical power — lift.
The variety in wing shapes among flying organic entities reflects variations to their
particular flight prerequisites. Taking off birds, similar to falcons and vultures, frequently
have long and expansive wings with a high perspective proportion (the proportion of
wingspan to average wing width). This plan limits drag and improves lift, permitting them
to cover huge distances with insignificant energy consumption. Interestingly, birds that
require quick and dexterous flight, like hawks, may have more limited wings with a lower
viewpoint proportion, improving mobility.

2. Drag: The Resistive Power Contradicting Movement
Sorts of Drag:
While lift is fundamental for defeating gravity, the going with power of drag acts contrary
to the course of movement and should be limited for effective flight. Drag emerges from
different sources, each requesting cautious thought in the plan and execution of wings.

Parasitic Drag:
Parasitic drag, otherwise called structure drag, results from the state of the flying living
being as it travels through the air. The smoothed out state of wings plans to limit
parasitic drag by decreasing the opposition experienced. Bugs, with their thin bodies
and smoothed out wings, embody this variation, permitting them to explore the air with
negligible opposition.

Initiated Drag:
Instigated drag is a result of lift age and is intently attached to the approach. At the point
when a living being builds its approach to create more lift, instigated drag additionally
increments. Adjusting the compromise among lift and prompted drag is critical for
accomplishing productive flight. Birds and bats have developed techniques, for
example, wing transforming and changes in flight act, to streamline this equilibrium and
diminish prompted drag.

Profile Drag:
Profile drag results from the contact between the wing's surface and the air. Smoother
surfaces, for example, those found in the quills of birds, assist with limiting profile drag.

Conversely, the membranous wings of bugs might have tiny designs that upset wind stream, decreasing profile drag.

Wing Morphology and Drag Decrease:
Wing morphology assumes a crucial part in drag decrease. The viewpoint proportion, wing stacking, and wingtip highlights add to the by and large streamlined proficiency of wings.

Angle Proportion:
The perspective proportion, characterized as the wingspan squared separated by the wing region, is a critical determinant of streamlined execution. High angle proportion wings, as found in gooney birds and other taking off birds, bring about lower prompted drag and expanded lift-to-drag proportions. This transformation is especially favorable for extremely long travel and energy-proficient floating.
Conversely, low perspective proportion wings, as seen in many flying predators and bats, are related with expanded mobility. These wings are appropriate for fast shifts in course and exact control during hunting or route through complex conditions.

Wing Stacking:
Wing stacking, the proportion of an organic entity's weight to its wing region, impacts its capacity to create lift. Low wing stacking, normal for birds with huge wings and generally low body weight, takes into consideration more slow flight speeds and upgraded lift age. High wing stacking, found in birds with more modest wings and more noteworthy body weight, is related with quicker flight speeds and expanded security.

Wingtip Elements:
The wingtips of flying organic entities contribute altogether to drag decrease. Wingtip vortices, produced as wind currents from the higher strain underneath the wing to the lower tension above, can prompt expanded instigated drag. To counter this, many flying living beings have developed wingtip elements, for example, winglets or improved wingtips.
Gooney birds, with their long and tight wings, are known for their productive taking off and decreased wingtip vortices. Likewise, airplane have integrated winglets to further develop eco-friendliness by limiting instigated drag.

3. Morphological Variations in Birds, Bugs, and Bats
Birds:
The variety of wing morphology in birds is a demonstration of the versatility of flight structures across environmental specialties. Taking off birds, like hawks and gooney birds, frequently have high viewpoint proportion wings for productive skimming.

Their long, expansive wings limit instigated drag, permitting them to cover huge distances with negligible exertion.

On the other hand, flying predators, similar to hawks, display lower perspective proportion wings, enhancing mobility for fast plunges and exact hunting. The compromise among wingspan and wing region is finely tuned to fulfill the particular needs of their hunting techniques.

Notwithstanding angle proportion, wing stacking fluctuates among bird species. High wing stacking, found in huge waterfowl and a few raptors, works with strong and stable flight. Alternately, low wing stacking portrays little larks, empowering them to float, flutter, and explore thick vegetation with spryness.

The wingtips of birds frequently highlight transformations to moderate drag. Gooney birds exhibit a rich arrangement with their long and slim wings, decreasing wingtip vortices during expanded taking off flights. Swifts, then again, have profoundly forked tail feathers that guide in limiting drag during fast elevated quests for bugs.

Bugs:

In the realm of bugs, where size and nimbleness are many times contrarily corresponding, wing morphology is a wonder of variation. The membranous wings of bugs are lightweight, taking into account fast and spry flight. Notwithstanding, this lightweight construction accompanies difficulties connected with toughness and strength.

Dragonflies, with their huge and diverse eyes, embody the adaptability of bug wings. Their wings are portrayed by an organization of veins that offers primary help. The venation design adds to the general strength of the wings, permitting dragonflies to perform gymnastic moves and catch prey mid-flight.

Butterflies, with their fragile and frequently beautiful wings, exhibit the unpredictable exchange among structure and capability. The wing sizes of butterflies fill numerous needs, including thermoregulation, cover, and optimal design. The scales diminish drag and add to the laminar progression of air over the wings, upgrading generally flight productivity.

Scarabs, a different gathering of bugs, have adjusted their forewings into elytra — a defensive covering that safeguards the membranous hindwings. While elytra give insurance, they likewise present a test for productive flight. Insects conquer this by unfurling their hindwings just during flight, limiting drag and enhancing streamlined execution.

Bats:
Bats, as the main warm blooded creatures fit for supported flight, show wing morphology that is unmistakable from the two birds and bugs. The lengthened fingers of bats help a dainty film, the patagium, making a wing structure that is both adaptable and productive.
The wing morphology of bats is adjusted for assorted environmental jobs. Bug eating bats frequently have long and thin wings, taking into account fast and deft flight, fundamental for catching equivocal prey. Organic product bats, then again, may have bigger wings with a higher viewpoint proportion, working with effective significant distance trip for searching across sweeping domains.
The adaptability of bat wings takes into account mind boggling control during flight. By adjusting the ebb and flow of the wing, bats can execute sharp turns, float set up, and explore complex conditions with accuracy. This versatility is especially apparent in the extraordinary flight styles of nectar-taking care of bats, which float close to blossoms to take care of.

4. Developmental Importance and Versatility
Developmental Importance:
The variety of wing morphology across flying living beings mirrors the transformative tensions and biological specialties that have formed their variations. The journey for energy productivity, mobility, and particular environmental jobs has driven the advancement of wings that are finely tuned to the particular necessities of every species.
The development of wings plays had a significant impact in the achievement and enhancement of flying organic entities. From the main bugs that took to the skies during the Carboniferous time frame to the different cluster of bird species that occupy practically every edge of the globe, the development of wings has been a dynamic and continuous cycle.
The change to controlled flight, a characterizing element of birds and bats, addresses a groundbreaking achievement throughout the entire existence of life on The planet. It took into account the colonization of new natural surroundings, escape from ground-based hunters, and the investigation of three-layered conditions. The versatility of wing morphology has been a vital calculate the transformative progress of these organic entities.

Flexibility:
The flexibility of wing morphology is clear in the combination of comparable arrangements in remotely related bunches confronting comparative difficulties. For instance, the smoothed out states of dolphins and sharks, albeit adjusted for life in the water, show similitudes to the streamlined standards found in flying organic entities.

This combination features the effectiveness of specific morphological elements in conquering actual difficulties.

On the other hand, the variety in wing morphology among firmly related species can be credited to specialty specialization and natural difference. Tribal species might have enhanced into various biological jobs, prompting the development of wings streamlined for explicit capabilities — whether it be significant distance taking off, quick ethereal pursuits, or drifting.

The fossil record gives experiences into the slow development of wings in different ancestries. Momentary fossils, like Archaeopteryx, offer looks into the phases of avian advancement, displaying the slow improvement of quills and the skeletal transformations that made ready for fueled flight. Additionally, the fossilized remaining parts of antiquated bugs uncover the steady changes in wing morphology that happened throughout topographical time.

Chapter 2
Masters of the Sky

The skies, tremendous and boundless, have been the material for a stunning showcase of life's most gifted pilots — birds. "Experts of the Sky" leaves on a complete excursion into the domain of avian greatness, disclosing the phenomenal transformations, ways of behaving, and natural jobs that characterize these ethereal maestros. From the grand soarers that explore immense distances no sweat to the coordinated trackers executing accuracy plunges, this investigation digs into the assorted universe of birds and their dominance of the skies.

1. Taking off Monsters: The Specialty of Easy Flight
Gooney birds: The Stupendous Pilots

The gooney bird, with its colossal wingspan and rich floating, remains as an image of dominance over the vast sea. This portion uncovers the privileged insights of gooney bird flight, investigating the physical variations that empower these amazing pilots to cover large number of miles with negligible energy use. From their effective utilization of dynamic taking off to the difficulties of life adrift, the gooney birds embody the specialty of taking off trip in the endlessness of the maritime span.

Vultures: The Flying Scroungers

Vultures, frequently misjudged and undervalued, feature astounding transformations for taking off flight and searching. This part dives into the remarkable wing morphology of vultures, their capacity to ride thermals with artfulness, and the significant biological job they play in cleaning environments. Notwithstanding their apparently easy flight, vultures face current difficulties, underscoring the sensitive harmony between their environmental significance and the dangers they experience.

2. Aeronautical Hunters: Accuracy in Flight and Hunting
Birds of prey: Experts of Speed and Spryness

Birds of prey, with their extraordinary speed and aeronautical ability, are the embodiment of avian trackers. This portion disentangles the mysteries behind the hawk's capacity to arrive at amazing paces during stoop plunges, hunting with unrivaled accuracy. From the life systems of their smoothed out wings to the job of vision in focusing on prey, hawks arise as obvious experts of the sky, mixing rate, deftness, and sharp faculties in a destructive blend.

Owls: Quiet Trackers of the Evening
The night sky is administered by the quiet and impressive trackers — owls. This segment investigates the extraordinary transformations of owls for nighttime predation, from their particular plumes for quiet trip to the momentous construction of their facial circles that improve sound limitation. The perplexing dance of owl flight, combined with their excellent vision and hearing, lays out a picture of dominance in low-light circumstances, offering a brief look into the mysteries of these mysterious nighttime hunters.

3. Accuracy Pilots: Transients and Significant Distance Fliers
Cold Terns: Heroes of Relocation
The Cold tern, a genuine yet surprising bird, holds the title of the longest transient excursion in the avian realm. This section follows the incredible movement of Cold terns, spreading over from the Icy to the Antarctic and back, and investigates the physiological variations that empower them to embrace this phenomenal excursion. The perplexing route abilities, the difficulties of significant distance flight, and the job of nature in this yearly odyssey shed light on the genuine authority of these accuracy pilots.

Hummingbirds: Elevated Aerialists and Nectar Specialists
In the domain of accuracy flight and dexterity, hummingbirds become the overwhelming focus. This part discloses the insider facts behind the hummingbird's amazing ability to float, quick moves, and concentrated taking care of strategies. From their elevated ability to burn calories to the extraordinary ball-and-attachment joint in their wings, hummingbirds exhibit the specialty of ethereal trapeze artistry and the coevolutionary hit the dance floor with the blossoms that give their life-supporting nectar.

4. Helpful Fliers: The Orchestra of Gathering Flight
Starlings: Aeronautical Ballet productions and Murmurations
The hypnotizing murmurations of starlings paint the sky with liquid examples, exhibiting the dazzling agreement of gathering flight. This section digs into the aggregate way of behaving of starlings, investigating the components that permit huge number of people to move as one. From the correspondence flags that coordinate their developments to the natural benefits of rushing, starlings represent the authority of helpful trip in the avian world.

Pelicans: Collaboration and Accuracy in Skimming Flight
Pelicans, with their enormous wings and synchronized flight designs, grandstand the specialty of helpful fishing through skimming flight.

This part investigates the life systems of pelican wings, their organized hunting techniques, and the significance of cooperation in getting a feast. The accuracy and proficiency of pelican skimming flight feature the advantages of cooperative endeavors chasing after food.

5. Vocal Virtuosos: The Language of the Skies
Songbirds: Tunes in Flight
Birdsong, an orchestra that reverberates through the skies, is a demonstration of the vocal virtuosity of specific avian species. Songbirds, prestigious for their captivating tunes, become the overwhelming focus in this section. The investigation dives into the physiological parts of songbird tune creation, the job of singing in romance and region guard, and the unpredictable association among vocalization and avian way of behaving.

Melodious Emulates: The Miracles of Warblers
Warblers, with their assorted collection of tunes, exhibit the limit with regards to vocal learning and mimicry. This segment unwinds the secrets of tune learning in birds, from the physical variations that empower mimicry to the social transmission of melody designs. Models from the avian world, including the mockingbird and the lyrebird, exhibit the unprecedented variety of vocal virtuosos and the social meaning of tune in their social orders.

6. Bosses of Impersonation: The Craft of Cover and Misdirection
Moths: Winged Deceptions in Disguise
Moths, with their enigmatic wing designs and tricky mimicry, grandstand the specialty of cover in the airborne domain. This portion investigates the transformative weapons contest among moths and their hunters, from mirroring leaves to looking like hazardous partners. The perplexing dance of double dealing, worked out in the visual orchestra of wing designs, uncovers the versatility of moths in exploring the difficulties of predation.

Butterflies: Winged Imaginativeness and Mimicry
Butterflies, prestigious for their energetic wing designs, participate in a fragile artful dance of mimicry and self-articulation. This part digs into the assorted systems utilized by butterflies, from imitating poisonous partners to showing complicated romance examples. The transformative meaning of wing shading and the environmental dance among butterflies and their hunters unfurl as a demonstration of the masterfulness of trickiness in the realm of winged ponders.

7. Gatekeepers of the Evening: Bats and the Privileged insights of Nighttime Flight

Bats: The Mammalian Pilots

Bats, the main warm blooded animals equipped for supported flight, divulge the mysteries of their nighttime authority. This portion investigates the extraordinary wing morphology of bats, from their stretched fingers to the adaptable films that empower dexterous flight. The echolocation ability of bats, their different natural jobs, and the difficulties looked by these gatekeepers of the night shed light on the momentous transformations that characterize their position in the nighttime skies.

8. Human Desires: From Icarus to the Skies of Tomorrow

Human Flight: The Quest for Icarian Dreams

The human interest with flight, from the legendary stories of Icarus to the spearheading accomplishments of flying, has been a demonstration of our getting through journey for the skies. This part follows the authentic achievements of human flight, from the primary sight-seeing balloon climb to the Wright siblings' fueled flight. The equals among avian and human flight, the mechanical developments that have impelled us into the elevated domain, and the continuous mission for investigation unfurl as a demonstration of the unstoppable soul of human goals.

Future Skylines: The Skies of Tomorrow

The investigation closes with a look toward the future skylines of flight and aviation. From bio-roused plan standards attracted from avian greatness to the potential for maintainable aeronautics, this part imagines the skies of tomorrow. The natural ramifications of human flight, the job of development in moderating ecological effect, and the cooperative endeavors toward an amicable conjunction with the avian world present a guide for the proceeded with investigation of the skies.

2.1 Avian excellence: exploring the diverse flying techniques of birds

The skies are the material whereupon birds paint a stunning embroidery of flight, displaying unmatched flying ability and dominance. Avian greatness in flight is a demonstration of the different transformations and flying methods that have developed across a bunch of animal varieties. From the easy taking off of raptors to the aerobatic moves of swifts, this investigation digs into the rich variety of flying procedures utilized by birds, unwinding the insider facts that permit them to explore the three-layered domain with unmatched ability.

1. Taking off Experts: Easy Coast and Extremely long Travel
Gooney birds: The Great Pilots

Among the taking off experts of the avian world, gooney birds stand apart as models of really long travel and proficient coasting. These seabirds, outfitted with an uncommon wingspan, grandstand the specialty of dynamic taking off — a procedure that bridles the energy from wind slopes over the vast sea. By capably utilizing the limit between air masses with various speeds, gooney birds cover large number of miles with negligible fluttering, saving energy for their broad processes looking for food.

The life structures of gooney bird wings, including a high perspective proportion and an ability to surprise to conform to shifting breeze conditions, adds to their dominance of dynamic taking off. This transformation permits gooney birds to ride the breeze for broadened periods, easily covering tremendous distances as they circumnavigate the globe. The blend of physical transformations and key utilization of wind designs represents the unrivaled extremely long travel accomplished by these fabulous pilots.

2. Accuracy Trackers: Flying Predation and Proficient Pursuits
Peregrine Birds of prey: Fast Stoop Jumps

In the domain of accuracy trackers, peregrine birds of prey are unparalleled in their dominance of rapid stoop plunges — a stunning presentation of ethereal deftness and deadly proficiency. Peregrines influence gravity to advance quickly during their jumps, arriving at surprising velocities of north of 240 miles each hour. The life structures of their wings, portrayed by pointed tips and a moderate viewpoint proportion, adds to their streamlined greatness, permitting them to execute exact and quick moves during pursuit.

The hunting technique of peregrines depends on extraordinary vision, empowering them to recognize prey from significant stretches. As they lock onto their objective, peregrines enter a controlled stoop jump, wrapping up their wings for smoothed out optimal design. This rapid drop finishes in a staggering strike, highlighting the momentous mix of visual sharpness and flying ability that characterizes their dominance of accuracy hunting.

3. Dynamic Stunt-devils: Flying Moves and Dexterity
Swifts: Bosses of Flying Aerobatic exhibition

Swifts, with their smooth and smoothed out bodies, become the dominant focal point as powerful aerialists of the avian world. These elevated virtuosos grandstand unrivaled deftness and accuracy in flight, executing mind boggling moves no sweat. Swifts are capable at flying low over territory, peddling bugs on the wing, and exploring complex conditions with excellent spatial mindfulness.

The life structures of swifts adds to their elevated gymnastics, highlighting long and thin wings, a short forked tail, and strong flight muscles.

This setup permits swifts to perform fast winds, turns, and flips, showing a degree of dexterity that is essential for catching subtle prey mid-flight. Their dominance of dynamic flight is additionally upgraded by the capacity to secure their wings in a shut situation during supported times of coasting, lessening drag and improving effectiveness.

4. Nighttime Guides: Quiet Flight and Low-Light Mastery
Horse shelter Owls: Quiet Trackers of the Evening

In the domain of nighttime flight, horse shelter owls arise as quiet trackers, using particular transformations for productive and silent flight. These flying predators have created one of a kind wing and plume structures that limit choppiness, permitting them to move toward their prey quietly in obscurity. The main edge of their essential plumes includes a serrated periphery, which upsets the wind stream and decreases the sound delivered during flight.

Stable owls' dependence on low-light circumstances requires excellent night vision, worked with by a high thickness of bar cells in their retinas. This transformation permits them to explore and chase successfully in obscurity. The cooperative energy between quiet flight and uplifted tangible discernment highlights the developmental dominance of horse shelter owls in the domain of nighttime route.

5. Floating Maestros: Accuracy Flight and Nectar Scrounging
Hummingbirds: Pros at Drifting

In the realm of drifting flight, hummingbirds are unrivaled maestros, exhibiting the capacity to suspend themselves in mid-air with astounding accuracy. The life structures of hummingbirds is adjusted for this exceptional flight style, including particular wing morphology, strong flight muscles, and fast wing beats that make lift and push. This mix of transformations permits hummingbirds to float before blossoms while benefiting from nectar.

The quick wing beats of hummingbirds, frequently surpassing 50 beats each second, create lift and empower them to keep a steady situation in the air. The deftness of their flight is additionally upgraded by the capacity to pivot their wings in a round trip, considering complicated moves like in reverse flight and fast shifts in course. Hummingbirds' dominance of drifting flight isn't just a demonstration of their versatility yet in addition an enamoring show of accuracy chasing food.

6. Agreeable Flyers: Synchronized Development and Group Elements
Starlings: Flying Ballet performances and Murmurations

In the domain of helpful flight, starlings take part in stunning ethereal ballet performances known as murmurations — an entrancing showcase of synchronized development that resists individual limits.

These herds of birds make liquid examples overhead, executing fast and facilitated course adjustments. The aggregate way of behaving of starlings is coordinated through viewable signs and correspondence, permitting them to answer as a bound together substance to outer improvements.

The capacity of starlings to move as one depends on the fast trade of data inside the herd. Individual birds change their flight way founded on the developments of their neighbors, making a flowing impact all through the murmuration. This synchronized conduct fills different needs, including hunter avoidance, data sharing, and possibly upgrading the productivity of scrounging. Starlings' dominance of agreeable flight features the intricacy of avian social elements in the elevated domain.

2.2 Comparative analysis of flight in different bird species

Flight, a characterizing element of birds, has developed into a heap of structures, each finely tuned to the particular necessities and natural specialties of various species. This near examination investigates the assorted transformations and flight methodologies that have arisen across the avian realm. From the taking off experts to the accuracy trackers, each bird species features a novel arrangement of physical, physiological, and conduct characteristics that add to their dominance of the skies.

1. Life systems of Flight: Wings, Muscles, and Skeletons
Gooney birds: Excellent Guides of the Untamed Sea

Gooney birds, known for their magnificent rising above the untamed sea, have unmistakable physical elements that add to their dominance of extremely long travel. Their wings are portrayed by a high viewpoint proportion — long wings comparative with their width — permitting them to cover tremendous distances with negligible fluttering effectively. The gooney bird's skeletal design is adjusted for perseverance, with a lightweight however hearty system that empowers supported trip over maritime territories.

The pectoral muscles of gooney birds, answerable for controlling their wings, are profoundly evolved to help expanded times of dynamic taking off. This variation, joined with a smoothed out body, empowers gooney birds to tackle wind designs over the untamed sea, covering great many miles looking for food. The near examination of gooney bird life structures features the specialization expected for productive significant distance trip in open conditions.

Peregrine Birds of prey: Accuracy Trackers overhead

Peregrine birds of prey, famous for their rapid stoop jumps during chases, show an alternate arrangement of physical variations equipped towards accuracy and nimbleness. Their wings are more limited and pointed, with a lower perspective proportion, considering fast shifts in course and exact moves during pursuit.

The hawk's skeletal construction is intended for speed, with variations like a lightweight however solid bone design.

The strong flight muscles of peregrine birds of prey are moved in the bosom region, giving the fundamental power to fast stoop plunges. Moreover, the design of their quills limits haul during fast drops. This near examination features the compromises in wing morphology and skeletal variations that empower peregrine birds of prey to succeed in the accuracy hunting methodologies normal for their species.

2. Flight Techniques: Taking off, Drifting, and Airborne Aerobatic exhibition
Red-followed Falcons: Taking off Subject matter experts

Red-followed birds of prey, normal raptors tracked down across various environments, are adroit at taking off flight. Their wide wings and high perspective proportion add to proficient skimming and taking off, making them pros at using warm flows. This flight methodology is appropriate for covering enormous domains while using insignificant energy.

Red-followed sells frequently use thermals — rising sections of warm air — to acquire elevation without fluttering their wings. By spiraling inside these updrafts, they can accomplish great levels and review extensive scenes for prey. The relative examination of flight methodologies in red-followed birds of prey stresses the job of taking off in improving energy effectiveness for enormous scope hunting and domain investigation.

Hummingbirds: Pros at Drifting Flight

Hummingbirds, on the opposite finish of the flight range, have developed to work in drifting flight — a momentous transformation that permits them to benefit from nectar from blossoms with unmatched accuracy. Their wing morphology is novel, highlighting a ball-and-attachment joint at the shoulder and a pivot at the elbow that considers a full scope of movement. This transformation, joined with quick wing beats, empowers hummingbirds to float in mid-air, removing nectar from blossoms with their specific bills. The pectoral muscles of hummingbirds are exceptionally evolved to help the quick and supported wing beats expected for drifting. Moreover, their digestion is astoundingly high, giving the energy expected to this enthusiastically requesting flight style. The near examination of hummingbird flight procedures highlights the specialization expected for floating, a strategy fundamental for getting to botanical assets.

Starlings: Helpful Elevated Ballet productions

Starlings take part in helpful flight, making entrancing murmurations that feature synchronized development for a terrific scope. Their flight procedure includes mind boggling coordination and correspondence inside the herd. The life structures of starlings upholds this agreeable way of behaving, with the capacity to change flight ways in light of obvious prompts from neighboring people.

The wings of starlings are adjusted for quick and light-footed moves, considering the liquid examples found in murmurations. The similar examination of flight methodologies in starlings features the significance of correspondence and composed development for the aggregate advantage of the group, whether it be for hunter avoidance or improved searching proficiency.

3. Natural Variations: Specialty Specialization and Living space Usage
Horse shelter Swallows: Nimble Flying Insectivores

Outbuilding swallows are profoundly nimble ethereal insectivores that have adjusted to an existence of hunting on the wing. Their thin, pointed wings and profoundly forked tail are appropriate for quick and exact ethereal moves, permitting them to get bugs in flight. The similar examination of horse shelter swallow life systems underlines the specialization for a particular environmental specialty — catching bugs in mid-air — and the job of flight variations in upgrading their searching proficiency.

Horse shelter swallows are known for their gymnastic flight, which incorporates dipping, jumping, and multifaceted examples during elevated attacks. Their smoothed out bodies and strong flight muscles empower them to execute these moves with striking dexterity. The biological transformation of stable swallows to an eating regimen of elevated bugs is complicatedly connected to their flight morphology, featuring the exchange among life systems and natural specialty specialization.

Woodpeckers: Extraordinary Flight Examples in Forested Conditions

Woodpeckers, albeit not known for expanded flights, grandstand remarkable flight designs adjusted to their arboreal way of life. Their life systems highlights solid and tough wings, taking into consideration short eruptions of non-stop trip between trees. The relative examination of woodpecker flight stresses the significance of mobility and brief distance trip in exploring thick forested conditions.

Woodpeckers depend on major areas of strength for them muscles and tail feathers for solidness during fast risings and plummets along tree trunks. Their flight designs are frequently described by undulating developments and short delays, mirroring the difficulties of exploring through a lush natural surroundings. The biological transformations of woodpeckers grandstand the variety of flight systems that have developed to fulfill the needs of explicit territories.

4. Social Variations: Romance Showcases and Transitory Excursions
Wilson's Kill: Airborne Romance Showcases

Wilson's kill, a shorebird, participates in elevated romance shows that include a progression of fabulous plunges and moves during flight. Their life structures is adjusted to help these mind boggling moves, with pointed wings and an unmistakable ethereal presentation.

The relative examination of Wilson's kill flight conduct highlights the job of flight transformations in romance ceremonies and the meaning of flying presentations in mate choice.

The romance showcases of Wilson's kill include rising flights, trailed by quick plunges with particular "winnowing" sounds created by the air racing through their essential plumes. These presentations feature their flying skills as well as act for the purpose of correspondence during the reproducing season. The conduct transformations in Wilson's kill flight feature the combination of trip into complex social cooperations.

Icy Terns: Long distance race Travelers

Cold terns attempt one of the longest transitory excursions in the avian world, covering huge number of miles between their Icy favorable places and Antarctic wintering regions. Their life structures and physiology are adjusted for perseverance flights, including long wings and a high perspective proportion that supports supported travel. The relative examination of Icy tern flight underscores the physiological transformations expected for perseverance during long distance race relocations.

Cold terns display wonderful navigational abilities, depending on divine signs, geomagnetic data, and ecological circumstances to explore across immense distances. Their capacity to cover massive distances during movement is a demonstration of the coordination of flight transformations, route, and perseverance. The environmental meaning of Icy tern relocations features the job of trip in getting to different territories and streamlining asset use.

2.3   Behavioral adaptations for aerial survival

Endurance in the elevated domain requests a complicated exchange of physical, physiological, and social transformations. While physical highlights like wings and plumes add to flight abilities, social transformations are similarly essential for exploring the unique difficulties of the skies. This investigation digs into the different systems utilized by different flying life forms, from birds to bugs and bats, to guarantee their ethereal endurance through multifaceted ways of behaving that upgrade scrounging, correspondence, route, and social collaborations.

1. Searching Procedures: Accuracy in Quest for Food
Swallows: Ethereal Gymnastics for Bug Catch

Swallows, prestigious for their ethereal trapeze artistry, utilize social transformations to upgrade rummaging productivity. These spry birds take part in modern flight designs, executing fast contorts, turns, and jumps to catch flying bugs with amazing accuracy. The long, pointed wings of swallows, combined with their smoothed out bodies, permit them to explore through the air with negligible opposition, displaying a particular rummaging methodology that benefits from their flight capacities.

Swallows frequently chase in gatherings, upgrading their searching accomplishment through helpful ways of behaving. By planning their developments, these birds make an ethereal expressive dance, crowding multitudes of bugs into concentrated regions where they can be proficiently caught. This social rummaging conduct works on individual accomplishment as well as shows the flexibility of swallows in improving food procurement through aggregate endeavors.

Dragonflies: Elevated Hunters with Accuracy Strikes
Dragonflies, bosses of elevated predation, display social variations that make them imposing trackers. Their huge compound eyes give all encompassing vision, permitting them to recognize prey with remarkable exactness. Dragonflies are known for their capacity to drift in mid-air, empowering them to evaluate their environmental factors and plan exact strikes on clueless bugs.
The hunting system of dragonflies includes catching prey during flight. Their extraordinary deftness permits them to take a different path quickly, chasing after and catching flying bugs with very much planned moves. The social variations of dragonflies exhibit the reconciliation of visual keenness, exact flight control, and vital preparation in improving their searching achievement.

2. Route and Relocation: Accuracy in Really long Travel
Ruler Butterflies: Exploring Across Landmasses
Ruler butterflies participate in one of the most noteworthy accomplishments of route — significant distance relocation across mainlands. The social transformations of rulers include a mix of inborn impulses and learned ways of behaving. In spite of their sensitive appearance, rulers attempt epic excursions, voyaging great many miles between their favorable places in North America and wintering destinations in Mexico. Rulers utilize a mix of divine signals, basically the place of the sun, and the World's attractive field for route. The capacity to make up for changes in the place of the sun during the day and keep a steady heading exhibits the accuracy in their transient way of behaving. Also, the utilization of ecological prompts, for example, milestones and wind designs, further adds to their capacity to explore across immense distances.

Cold Terns: Navigational Skill in Cross-country Movement
Cold terns, known for their cross-country relocations between Icy favorable places and Antarctic wintering regions, exhibit remarkable navigational ability. These birds participate in a yearly full circle relocation that covers amazing distances, exploring across seas and mainlands. The conduct transformations of Icy terns remember dependence for different navigational prompts and the capacity to change their course founded on evolving conditions.

Icy terns utilize heavenly signs, like the place of the sun and stars, for route. Their transient way of behaving is likewise impacted by geomagnetic data, permitting them to keep up with course even without visual milestones. The accuracy in Icy tern route features the many-sided exchange between natural navigational senses and the capacity to adjust to ecological factors during extremely long travel.

3. Social Ways of behaving: Collaboration and Correspondence in the Skies
Starlings: Aeronautical Ballet performances and Aggregate Insight

Starlings take part in hypnotizing murmurations, aggregate presentations of synchronized flight that make liquid examples overhead. These ethereal ballet performances include large number of people moving as one, making a stunning exhibition. The conduct variations of starlings for aggregate flight feature the significance of collaboration and correspondence in improving step by step processes for surviving.

The planned developments of starlings in murmurations fill different needs, including hunter avoidance, data sharing about food sources, and upgrading rummaging productivity. The capacity to answer quickly to viewable signals from adjoining people and change flight ways appropriately features the aggregate insight of starlings. This social conduct upgrades their possibilities of endurance as well as epitomizes the flexibility of birds in involving coordinated effort as a method for surviving.

Bats: Echolocation for Nighttime Route

Bats, the main well evolved creatures fit for supported flight, depend on echolocation as an essential social variation for exploring in obscurity. These nighttime animals emanate high-recurrence sound waves and tune in for the reverberations, permitting them to make an itemized mental guide of their environmental factors. Echolocation is fundamental for hunting prey, staying away from impediments, and exploring complex conditions during night flights.

The social transformations of bats for echolocation include changing the recurrence and power of discharged sounds in view of their environmental factors. This complex framework empowers them to distinguish prey, like bugs, by the reverberations created when sound waves skip off objects. The accuracy in their echolocation conduct highlights the significance of hear-able prompts in the airborne endurance of nighttime fliers.

4. Romance Showcases: Aeronautical Customs for Conceptive Achievement
Wilson's Kill: Airborne Romance Customs

Wilson's kill, shorebirds known for their unmistakable ethereal romance presentations, show conduct transformations that assume a vital part in regenerative achievement.

During the rearing season, male kills rise very high and perform fantastic plunges, making an interesting winnowing sound by changing their tail feathers. These ethereal showcases act for the purpose of drawing in expected mates.

The conduct variations of Wilson's kill for romance customs include the actual exhibition of flying presentations as well as the capacity to alter their flight conduct to deliver explicit acoustic signs. The winnowing sound, made via air hurrying through particular tail feathers, conveys data about the wellness and power of the showing male. This social procedure upgrades the possibilities of fruitful mate choice and adds to the continuation of their species.

Chapter 3
Beyond Feathers – Insect Aeronautics

In the huge embroidered artwork of the regular world, bugs arise as exceptional pilots, opposing the cutoff points forced by their little size. Past the polish of quills that describes birds, bugs explore the skies with perplexing wings, showing flight related ability that matches their bigger airborne partners. This investigation dives into the wonders of bug flight, revealing the physical, physiological, and conduct transformations that empower these diminutive pilots to overcome the three-layered domain.

1. Winged Marvels: The Variety of Bug Wings
Creepy crawlies: Elytra and Authority of Accuracy Flight

Creepy crawlies, with their forewings changed into solidified covers known as elytra, feature a remarkable way to deal with flight. The elytra give security to the sensitive hindwings underneath, filling in as a defensive safeguard when not being used. During flight, scarabs unfurl their hindwings and participate in a style of flight portrayed by its accuracy and soundness.

The elytra of creepy crawlies, regardless of their apparently awkward nature, add to streamlined proficiency. The synchronized development of elytra and hindwings permits creepy crawlies to explore with momentous dexterity, making them adroit fliers in different territories. This part investigates the complexities of scarab flight, underscoring the double reason plan of elytra and the developmental benefits they give.

Dragonflies: Experts of Controlled Flight

Dragonflies, old bugs that have graced the skies for a long period of time, epitomize the dominance of controlled flight. Their four prolonged wings, each controlled autonomously by strong flight muscles, permit dragonflies to execute complex moves with remarkable accuracy. The capacity to move each wing autonomously empowers dragonflies to drift, dart, and take an alternate route quickly, displaying the readiness gave by their wing structure.

The intricate wing developments of dragonflies are coordinated by a refined arrangement of muscles and nerves. This segment dives into the life systems of dragonfly wings and the multifaceted coordination expected for their great flight abilities. From hunting to romance presentations, dragonflies influence their fueled trip to explore and flourish in different environments.

2. The Optimal design of Little Flight: Difficulties and Arrangements
Butterflies: The Fragile Dance of Flight

Butterflies, with their agile and apparently easy flight, show the fragile dance of smaller than usual pilots. The wings of butterflies, canvassed in scales that add to their lively varieties, are a wonder of the two feel and capability. The complex examples on butterfly wings fill various needs, from species acknowledgment to hunter prevention. The streamlined features of butterfly flight include a mix of wing morphology, wingbeat recurrence, and body mechanics. This segment investigates the variations that permit butterflies to accomplish lift and mobility. The job of wing adaptability, the exceptional system of wing applauding during departure, and the energy-productive coasting methods of butterflies add to their prosperity as light-footed and fragile fliers.

Hoverflies: The Specialty of Floating

Hoverflies, frequently confused with honey bees because of their mimicry, succeed in the specialty of floating flight. Their capacity to suspend themselves in mid-air with momentous solidness is a demonstration of the accuracy of their flight transformations. Hoverflies assume urgent parts as pollinators, and their floating abilities permit them to get to nectar from blossoms with unmatched precision.

The optimal design of floating trip in hoverflies include fast wing beats, particular flight muscles, and a one of a kind system known as the "applaud and throw." This segment disentangles the complexities of hoverfly flight, underlining the variations that empower them to keep a steady situation in the air while scavenging for nectar. The exchange of wing morphology and flight mechanics in hoverflies exhibits the flexibility of scaled down pilots.

3. The Energetics of Flight: Difficult exercise in the Air
Mosquitoes: The Covert Fliers

Mosquitoes, notorious for their job as sickness vectors, are additionally noteworthy in their capacity to explore the air with secrecy and accuracy. The lengthened and slim life structures of mosquitoes, including their long proboscis, adds to their streamlined productivity. Mosquitoes take part in a novel sort of flight called "rippling," which permits them to explore through thick vegetation and move toward has without recognition.

The energetics of mosquito flight include a sensitive harmony between the energy consumed during flight and the requirement for proficient rummaging. This part investigates the transformations that empower mosquitoes to participate in subtle flight, featuring the significance of their flight capacities in both endurance and propagation. The developmental compromises in mosquito flight variations highlight the mind boggling exchange among energetics and natural techniques.

Insects: Public Flight and Settlement Development
Insects, known for their profoundly coordinated social orders, take part in an extraordinary period of public flight known as the marital flight. During this period, winged conceptive insects get off the ground to mate and lay out new provinces. The synchronized rise of winged subterranean insects, frequently set off by ecological prompts, grandstands the collective idea of this flying occasion.
The energetics of insect flight include the singular endeavors of winged reproductives as well as the aggregate objectives of laying out new provinces. This part dives into the elements of marital trips in subterranean insects, underlining the jobs of wing morphology, natural triggers, and the many-sided coordination expected for effective state extension. The versatile meaning of shared trip in subterranean insects gives bits of knowledge into the intricacies of conceptive systems in bug social orders.

4. From Pheromones to Move: Correspondence in Flying Domains
Bumble bees: Waggle Dance and Aggregate Route
Bumble bees, famous for their perplexing correspondence frameworks, expand their correspondence into the airborne domain through the waggle dance. This dance, performed by working drones in the hive, passes on data about the area of food sources or potential settling destinations. The direction and span of the dance give exact spatial data, permitting different individuals from the hive to explore to the imparted area.
The correspondence techniques of bumble bees include deciphering the many-sided data conveyed by the dance and changing flight designs appropriately. This segment investigates the job of the waggle dance in aggregate route, featuring the versatile meaning of this flying correspondence framework in enhancing rummaging productivity and asset use.

Fireflies: Bioluminescent Motioning in the Night Sky
Fireflies, with their hypnotizing bioluminescent presentations, take part in flying correspondence to work with mating. The musical glimmers of light discharged by male fireflies act as signs to draw in responsive females. The coordination of these bioluminescent signs inside a populace adds to the synchronization of mating conduct.
The correspondence techniques of fireflies include the exact timing of light emanations, guaranteeing that signs are adjusted inside a populace. This segment digs into the components behind firefly bioluminescence and the specific tensions that have molded this novel type of airborne correspondence. The transformation of involving light signals in the obscured skies highlights the assorted manners by which bugs impart for regenerative achievement.

5. Ethereal Designers: Settling and Conceptive Techniques
Wasps: Paper Draftsmen in the Air

Wasps, proficient manufacturers and modelers, take part in aeronautical development to make complex paper homes. The development of flying homes includes the assortment of plant filaments, which are bitten into a mash and formed into the primary parts of the home. The design abilities of wasps add to the conceptive outcome of the province, giving haven to creating posterity and an incorporated area for public exercises.

The settling systems of wasps include a blend of conduct variations, including the development of various home sorts relying upon the species. This segment investigates the aeronautical design of wasp homes, featuring the transformative meaning of their settling ways of behaving. The mutual idea of wasp settlements and the versatility of settling methodologies add to the outcome of these elevated draftsmen.

Termites: Upward Development through Alates

Termites, frequently connected with underground environments, participate in a striking period of elevated dispersal known as the winged stage. During this stage, winged conceptive termites get off the ground to lay out new provinces. The synchronized development of termite alates, set off by ecological circumstances, takes into consideration mass dispersal and builds the possibilities of effective state foundation. The settling procedures of termites include the aeronautical dispersal of alates as well as the resulting development of underground homes. This segment dives into the conceptive procedures of termites, stressing the job of elevated dispersal in growing state regions. The flexibility of termite provinces to both underground and aeronautical natural surroundings highlights the adaptability of their settling ways of behaving.

3.1   Insect flight mechanisms and their unique adaptations

In the domain of flight, bugs stand apart as momentous pilots, exhibiting dexterity, accuracy, and adaptability that challenge the customary limits of elevated abilities. This investigation digs into the complexities of bug flight instruments, disclosing the amazing variations that empower these small animals to explore the air with unmatched productivity. From wing morphology to muscle mechanics, this excursion into the universe of bug flight uncovers the miracles of their extraordinary transformations.

1. The Advancement of Wings: Variety in Structure and Capability
Transformative Beginnings of Bug Wings

The development of bug wings is an enamoring story of transformation and advancement. These designs, extraordinary to the bug class, play had a crucial impact in the achievement and expansion of this unimaginably different gathering.

The beginnings of bug wings stay a subject of logical request, with speculations proposing that they might have developed from familial designs that supported equilibrium or temperature guideline.

The changeability in wing morphology across bug orders reflects different environmental transformations. From the membranous wings of dragonflies to the solidified elytra of creepy crawlies, the transformative excursion of bug wings has prompted a variety of structures custom fitted to explicit necessities. This segment investigates the transformative starting points and versatile meaning of bug wings, featuring the amazing variety that has emerged through large number of long stretches of regular determination.

Wing Morphology and Usefulness

The different types of bug wings are unpredictably connected to their capabilities in flight and endurance. The two essential kinds of bug wings are the forewings (tegmina) and hindwings, which can display a scope of morphologies. Dragonflies, for instance, have lengthened and straightforward wings that empower fast and deft flight, while insects have solidified elytra that serve both defensive and streamlined capabilities. The venation designs on bug wings are one more part of their morphology that adds to flight proficiency. The complex organization of veins offers underlying help and characterizes the general state of the wing. This segment investigates the connection between wing morphology and usefulness, underlining how variations in structure permit bugs to address the particular difficulties of their surroundings.

2. The Force of Muscles: Accuracy in Flight Moves
Non-stop Flight Muscles: A Unique Force to be reckoned with

Bug flight is controlled by non-stop flight muscles, an extraordinary and exceptionally specific framework that separates them from vertebrate fliers. These muscles, connected straightforwardly to the wings, contract and unwind quickly to drive wing development. The withdrawal of these muscles abbreviates the chest, making the wings move descending, while unwinding permits the wings to move up. This system, known as nonconcurrent flight muscle constriction, empowers the fast wing beats normal for bug flight.

The effectiveness of non-stop flight muscles lies in their capacity to contract and unwind at high frequencies, permitting bugs to accomplish amazing wing beat rates. This transformation is significant for the floating, fast moves, and supported flights that numerous bugs participate in. This segment digs into the mechanics of non-stop flight muscles, underscoring their part in giving the power and accuracy important for the assorted flight ways of behaving displayed by bugs.

Backhanded Flight Muscles: Upgrading Mobility

A few bugs, like honey bees and wasps, have an extra arrangement of muscles known as backhanded flight muscles. Dissimilar to the non-stop flight muscles, these are not joined to the wings but rather are rather associated with the exoskeleton. Roundabout flight muscles assume a part in modifying the state of the chest, by implication impacting wing development.

The presence of roundabout flight muscles improves the mobility of specific bug species. By tweaking the thoracic shape, bugs can change the point of their wings and upgrade lift during flight. This part investigates the double muscle frameworks utilized by bugs, underscoring the collaboration among immediate and aberrant flight muscles that adds to their momentous elevated capacities.

3. Flight Control: Exploring the Three-Layered Domain

Wing Verbalization and Adaptability

Bug wings, regardless of their sensitive appearance, are wonders of designing that take into account perplexing control of flight. The explanation and adaptability of wings assume an essential part in accomplishing exact moves. The capacity to adjust wing shape and direction adds to the adaptability of bug flight, permitting them to drift, coast, and take a different path effortlessly.

Wing adaptability is accomplished through the presence of joints and films that give a scope of movement. Dragonflies, for instance, can change the point of their wings autonomously, empowering quick course adjustments during flight. This segment investigates the components of wing verbalization and adaptability, featuring the job of these transformations in upgrading the control and readiness of bug flight.

In-flight Changes: Answering Changing Circumstances

Bugs should explore a powerful flying climate, answering unexpected changes in wind, temperature, and obvious signs. The capacity to make continuous changes during flight is significant for their endurance and achievement. Bugs accomplish this through tangible input systems that illuminate them about their spatial direction and ecological circumstances.

This part dives into the tangible transformations that permit bugs to make in-flight changes. Mechanoreceptors on the wings give data about wind stream and wing position, while viewable prompts empower bugs to explore and stay away from impediments. The mix of tactile criticism with quick engine reactions guarantees that bugs can adjust to evolving conditions, displaying the flexibility and versatility of their flight control systems.

4. Energetics of Flight: Difficult exercise in the Air
Metabolic Requests of Flight

Flight is a vivaciously requesting movement, and bugs have advanced techniques to adjust the metabolic expenses related with supported aeronautical moves. The high-recurrence wing beats and fast muscle withdrawals expected for flight request a nonstop stock of energy. Bugs have adjusted their metabolic cycles to fulfill these needs, upgrading energy usage during flight productively.

This part investigates the metabolic transformations that empower bugs to support flight. The dependence on oxygen consuming digestion, productive supplement use, and variations in flight muscle structure add to the general proficiency of bug flight. The developmental compromises between energy consumption and regenerative achievement highlight the significance of energy the executives in the existence of flying bugs.

Flight and Scrounging Systems

Scrounging in the air presents novel difficulties, and bugs have created specific procedures to advance their energy use during flight. Hoverflies, for instance, participate in a way of behaving known as "trap-lining," where they visit a succession of blossoms in an anticipated example. This system limits the energy costs related with consistent drifting, permitting them to boost scavenging effectiveness.

This part dives into the scavenging transformations that bugs utilize during flight. From trap-covering to effective route of botanical scenes, bugs feature a variety of methodologies that balance the requests of trip with the requirement for asset procurement. The multifaceted interchange between flight energetics and rummaging ways of behaving features the flexibility of bugs to assorted environmental specialties.

5. Past Flight: Flying Variations for Endurance
Wing-Related Ways of behaving: Correspondence and Protection

Notwithstanding their essential capability in flight, bug wings assume parts in correspondence, protection, and thermoregulation. Wing-related ways of behaving, for example, wing flicking in mosquitoes or wing drumming in specific honey bees, act as correspondence signals inside populaces. These ways of behaving are frequently connected with romance customs, domain foundation, or cautioning signals.

Wings likewise add to guard systems in specific bugs. Grasshoppers, for instance, utilize their wings for frighten shows, utilizing abrupt and uproarious developments to deflect likely hunters. This segment investigates the multi-layered jobs of bug wings past flight, underlining how these transformations add to their general endurance and natural collaborations.

Disguise and Mimicry: Aeronautical Techniques for Endurance
Disguise and mimicry are boundless techniques utilized by bugs to avoid hunters or gain benefits in predation. A few bugs, like stick bugs, have wings that look like leaves or twigs, giving compelling cover against foundations like foliage. Others, similar to specific butterflies, use wing examples to impersonate the presence of poisonous or unpalatable species, acquiring security through trickiness.

This part digs into the airborne transformations of disguise and mimicry, underscoring the job of wings in these step by step processes for surviving. The transformative weapons contest among hunters and prey has driven the improvement of mind boggling designs and morphological variations, displaying the variety of strategies utilized by bugs to flourish in their particular environments.

3.2 The role of wing shape, size, and wing-beat frequency in insect flight

In the charming domain of bug flight, achievement is complicatedly woven into the texture of wing variations. The set of three of wing shape, size, and wing-beat recurrence frames the foundation of their ethereal ability, empowering these small scale pilots to explore different conditions with exceptional accuracy. This investigation digs into the transaction of wing morphology, size varieties, and the cadenced beat of wings, divulging the nuanced job every component plays in the elements of bug flight.

1. Wing Shape: Chiseling the Air
Elytra, Membranous Wings, and Then some
The variety of wing shapes across bug species mirrors an embroidery of developmental variations custom fitted to explicit environmental specialties. Bugs, with their defensive elytra, grandstand a wing shape that joins usefulness and insurance. Elytra act as defensive covers for membranous hindwings, unfurling during trip to uncover fragile designs underneath.

The smoothed out wings of dragonflies, portrayed by prolongation and straightforwardness, embody an efficiently productive plan. These wings, combined with the capacity to move autonomously, empower dragonflies to participate in quick and lithe flight. The development of different wing shapes is a demonstration of the versatile reactions of bugs to environmental difficulties, featuring the significance of wing morphology in chiseling the air around them.

Butterfly Wings: Masterfulness in Flight
Butterflies, eminent for their fragile and many-sided wing designs, embody the imaginativeness that can rise out of wing shape variations.

The expansive, level wings of butterflies add to their sluggish and agile flight, permitting them to float and coast with class. Wing venation, the plan of veins that structure mind boggling designs on butterfly wings, further upgrades their streamlined effectiveness. The different states of butterfly wings serve practical as well as open jobs. Romance showcases, species acknowledgment, and hunter prevention are much of the time interceded through the dynamic tones and examples on butterfly wings. This part investigates how the state of butterfly wings is a unique interchange of structure and capability, exhibiting the multifaceted harmony among feel and flight effectiveness.

2. Wing Size: Adjusting Lift and Burden
Little Wonders: The Benefit of Little Wings

In the realm of bug flight, size matters, however not in the manner in which one could anticipate. Numerous bugs, regardless of their small height, gloat wings that are relatively huge comparative with their body size. This variation isn't a mystery however an essential reaction to the streamlined difficulties looked by little fliers. Little wings, comparative with weight, improve mobility and empower quick course adjustments. Hoverflies, for example, feature the benefits of little wings through their capacity to drift in mid-air with astounding strength. The decreased wing stacking, the proportion of body weight to wing region, permits hoverflies to explore many-sided flower scenes with accuracy. This part digs into the transformations related with little wing sizes, underscoring the compromises that add to the outcome of these small wonders in flight.

The Coasting Game: Bigger Wings for Bigger Flyers

On the other hand, a few bugs, like specific butterflies and moths, embrace an alternate procedure by utilizing bigger wings comparative with their body size. Bigger wings offer benefits concerning skimming capacities and supported flight. The expanded surface region takes into account further developed lift, empowering these bigger flyers to cover longer distances with less energy use.

The swallowtail butterfly, with its rich and lengthened wings, embodies the benefits of bigger wings for floating. The capacity to take off on warm updrafts and cover extensive domains adds to the biological progress of these bigger winged bugs. This segment investigates how bigger wings work with coasting and supported flight, giving experiences into the versatile procedures related with various wing sizes.

3. Wing-Beat Recurrence: The Musical Dance of Flight
High-Recurrence Beats: Spryness in real life

The quick and cadenced beating of bug wings is an entrancing dance, a critical part of their flight variations. Wing-beat recurrence, estimated in beats each second, changes broadly among various bug species and is firmly connected to their flight ways of behaving.

High-recurrence wing beats add to readiness, permitting bugs to execute quick moves, drift set up, and take part in accuracy flight.

The hummingbird sell moth, with its honey bee imitating appearance, epitomizes the nimbleness related with high-recurrence wing beats. The quick shuddering of wings empowers these bugs to drift close to blossoms while searching for nectar. This segment investigates the variations related with high-recurrence wing beats, stressing the powerful interaction between wing movement and flight spryness.

Without rushing: Low-Recurrence Beats for Perseverance

Conversely, a few bugs embrace a system of low-recurrence wing beats, focusing on perseverance over fast moves. This transformation is much of the time saw in species participated in significant distance relocation or supported flight. The ruler butterfly, famous for its amazing movements across mainlands, exhibits the upsides of low-recurrence wing beats for covering huge distances.

The gradual wing beats of ruler butterflies add to their capacity to travel large number of miles during relocation. This segment dives into the transformations related with low-recurrence wing beats, featuring the compromises among dexterity and perseverance with regards to bug flight. The musical beat of wings, whether quick or intentional, structures the heartbeat of bug flight systems.

4. Cooperative energy of Wing Transformations: Flight Advancement

The Composite Picture: Incorporating Wing Highlights

The effectiveness of bug flight rises up out of the consistent mix of wing shape, size, and wing-beat recurrence. Species-explicit blends of these highlights enhance trip for specific environmental specialties and ways of behaving. The hawkmoth, with its smoothed out body, enormous wings, and fast wing beats, epitomizes the collaboration of these variations, taking into consideration exact drifting and nectar extraction.

This part investigates contextual analyses of bug species that represent the coordination of wing transformations. From the accuracy of dragonfly trip to the perseverance of ruler butterfly relocations, the composite picture uncovers the complicated manners by which wing morphology and wing-beat elements merge to shape fruitful flight systems. The improvement of flight, etched by a long period of time of development, highlights the versatility and flexibility of bug pilots.

3.3 The evolutionary arms race between insects and their predators

In the many-sided embroidery of nature, a continuous show unfurls — a dance of transformation, endurance, and rivalry known as the developmental weapons contest. No place is this dance more strikingly organized than in the connections among bugs and their hunters. North of millions of years, a unique transaction of developmental powers has formed the systems and counterstrategies utilized by the two players.

This investigation dives into the subtleties of the developmental weapons contest, uncovering the clever transformations that bugs and their hunters have created as they continued looking for endurance.

1. The Beginnings of the Weapons contest: An Old Contention
Basic Battles: The Development of Bug Predation

The developmental weapons contest among bugs and their hunters has old roots, extending back to the rise of bugs as a predominant and different gathering on The planet. As bugs developed to take advantage of a bunch of natural specialties, they became both imposing contenders and captivating prey for different hunters.

In the early sections of this continuous adventure, the particular strain applied by hunters inclined toward bugs with versatile attributes that presented security or upgraded their capacity to avoid catch. All the while, hunters advanced attributes that permitted them to turn out to be more viable trackers. This corresponding system set up for a powerful weapons contest that would shape the directions of incalculable bug and hunter genealogies.

2. Methodologies of Duplicity: Mimicry and Disguise
Mirroring Risk: Batesian Mimicry

One of the cunning methodologies that bugs have advanced because of predation is mimicry. Batesian mimicry is a peculiarity where an innocuous or tasteful animal varieties develops to look like a harmful or risky model, dissuading expected hunters. This mimicry is a tricky methodology that takes advantage of the learned repugnance of hunters to hurtful or harmful prey.

For example, the emissary butterfly imitates the presence of the harmful ruler butterfly, acquiring security from avian hunters that have figured out how to keep away from the ruler's poisonousness. This segment investigates the complexities of Batesian mimicry, underlining the transformative benefit it gives to bugs despite predation.

Mixing In: Mysterious Tinge and Cover

Disguise is one more developmental reaction that bugs have created to sidestep recognition by hunters. Mysterious hue permits bugs to mix consistently into their environmental factors, making them almost undetectable to hunters. This variation is especially common in species that occupy conditions with mind boggling and differed vegetation.

Models incorporate stick bugs that look like twigs or bark, and moths with wing designs that copy the surface of tree covering. The developmental weapons contest has driven the refinement of these disguise methodologies, as hunters with intense visual sharpness apply determination strain on bugs to upgrade their capacity to remain unnoticed just by being casual.

This part dives into the job of disguise in the transformative weapons contest, featuring the fragile harmony among camouflage and location.

3. Substance Fighting: Poisons and Protective Mixtures
Sequestering Poisons: Substance Protections in Bugs
Bugs have advanced an arms stockpile of synthetic safeguards, creating poisons or cautious mixtures that discourage or hurt hunters. This methodology, known as compound fighting, is a demonstration of the powerful idea of the weapons contest among bugs and their hunters. A few bugs orchestrate poisonous mixtures themselves, while others sequester poisons from their current circumstance.

For instance, the bombardier bug can create a harmful and extremely hot synthetic splash that it discharges as a safeguard system. The ruler butterfly, in its larval stage, sequesters poisonous mixtures from its milkweed have plants, making it unpalatable to numerous hunters. This segment investigates the variety of compound guards in bugs, featuring the coevolutionary elements that drive the refinement of these cautious systems.

Cautioning Signs: Aposematism and Legitimate Promoting
In light of the compound protections of bugs, a hunters have developed obstruction or resistance to these poisons. In any case, in an entrancing turn, certain bugs have developed cautioning signs to promote their poisonousness — a peculiarity known as aposematism. Brilliant varieties, striking examples, or particular markings act as obvious prompts to possible hunters, flagging that the bug is outfitted with synthetic protections. The exemplary model is the aposematic hue of many toxic substance dart frogs in tropical rainforests. Additionally, a few caterpillars and grown-up butterflies utilize advance notice signs to hinder would-be hunters. This segment dives into the universe of aposematism, investigating how legitimate promoting of poisonousness adds to the developmental weapons contest and the elements of hunter prey associations.

4. Mechanical Protections: Defensively covered Exoskeletons and Spines
An Exoskeletal Stronghold: Reinforced Guards in Bugs
The exoskeleton, an unbending outer covering, gives bugs a considerable mechanical protection against hunters. This exoskeletal stronghold fills in as both an actual hindrance and an underlying scaffolding for the bug's body. The transformative weapons contest has driven the advancement of exoskeletal highlights that improve assurance and endurance.

Bugs, with their solidified elytra, represent the force of a shielded exoskeleton. This segment investigates the mechanical guards managed the cost of by the exoskeleton, stressing how its design has developed to endure predation pressure.

The complicated harmony between weight, adaptability, and sturdiness in the exoskeleton mirrors the continuous weapons contest among bugs and their hunters.

Spines, Thistles, and Prickles: Protective Device

Past the exoskeleton, a few bugs have developed extra guarded structures as spines, thistles, or prickles. These transformations act as actual impediments, making it trying for hunters to deal with or consume the bug. Now and again, these designs may likewise be outfitted with poisons, adding an extra layer of protection.

Caterpillars of specific butterfly species, for instance, highlight spines that are sharp as well as covered with disturbing or harmful substances. This part investigates the variety of guarded contraption in bugs, featuring how these designs have developed in light of the specific tensions applied by hunters.

5. Social Departures: Surprising Showcases and Interruptions

Alarm Strategies: Abrupt Developments and Uproarious Clamors

In the weapons contest among bugs and their hunters, social variations assume a pivotal part. A few bugs have developed frightening showcases or ways of behaving that surprise hunters, giving the bug a chance to get away. Surprise strategies frequently include unexpected developments, boisterous commotions, or showcases that make a flashing interruption.

Grasshoppers, for example, may utilize their strong rear legs to take abrupt and surprising jumps when compromised. This abrupt development alarms expected hunters, permitting the grasshopper to get away from before the hunter can respond. This segment investigates the different manners by which bugs utilize frighten strategies as a social break system, displaying the inventiveness of their cautious collection.

Distraction Strategies: Mimicry and Conciliatory Parts

Certain bugs make conduct safeguards a stride further by utilizing fake strategies. This can include mimicry, where a bug impersonates the appearance or conduct of another thing to redirect the consideration of a hunter. Moreover, a few bugs have developed conciliatory parts that can be shed or forfeited to divert or confound a hunter.

In the domain of mimicry, the katydid, with its leaf-mirroring appearance, represents the specialty of redirection. A few bugs, similar to the glorious hopping bug, may drop a leg whenever got by a hunter, permitting them to escape while the hunter is quickly busy with the disposed of appendage. This segment dives into the universe of conduct avoids, investigating how bugs use mimicry and conciliatory strategies in their continuous battle for endurance.

Chapter 4
Flying Mammals – Bats in the Limelight

In the huge breadth of the animals of the world collectively, one gathering of well evolved creatures stands apart for its noteworthy variation to the skies - bats. These winged marvels have become amazing at flight, developing remarkable qualities that permit them to explore the night skies with unmatched accuracy. This investigation digs into the universe of flying warm blooded animals, placing bats at the center of attention as we disentangle the complexities of their life structures, physiology, conduct, and biological importance.

1. Transformative Wonders: The Starting points of Bat Flight
Taking to the Skies: An Early Transformative Jump
The development of flight is an achievement that has been accomplished by just a limited handful gatherings in the set of all animals, and bats address perhaps of the most uncommon model. Not at all like birds, which are their nearest flying family members, bats take care of a remarkable wing structure - extended fingers by a flimsy layer of skin, making a wing structure known as the patagium.
This segment investigates the transformative wonders that prompted the improvement of bat flight. Fossil proof gives bits of knowledge into the early variations that set before bats the way to becoming bosses of the skies. From their unassuming starting points to the assorted exhibit of bat species we see today, the transformative excursion of bats features the surprising variations that have permitted them to overcome the aeronautical domain.

2. Winged Designers: The Life systems of Bat Flight
The Patagium: A Winged Film of Accuracy
Key to the life systems of bat flight is the patagium, the meager film of skin that reaches out between extended fingers and interfaces with the body, legs, and tail. This winged construction permits bats to accomplish a degree of mobility and accuracy that is unequaled among vertebrates. The patagium is a demonstration of the unpredictable design that empowers bats to explore through the air with mind blowing spryness.
This segment dives into the subtleties of the patagium, investigating how varieties in wing morphology add to various flight styles among bat species.

From the long and thin wings of quick flying species to the expansive wings of species adjusted for slow and floating flight, the variety of wing structures mirrors the versatile radiation of bats into different environmental specialties.

Muscles and Joints: Calibrating Flight Elements
In the background of bat flight is a mind boggling arrangement of muscles and joints that work as one to tweak flight elements. The muscles controlling the developments of the wings are amazingly advanced, permitting bats to execute mind boggling moves like quick turns, jumps, and drifting. The joints in the fingers and wrists are adaptable, giving the scope of movement vital for the nuanced control of wing shape.
This segment investigates the solid and skeletal transformations that support bat flight. The powerful interchange between muscle strength and adaptability, combined with the accuracy of joint developments, empowers bats to accomplish the aerobatic accomplishments that characterize their aeronautical ability. Understanding the complexities of bat life structures reveals insight into the biomechanics of their flight abilities.

3. Echolocation: The Sonar Orchestra of Bat Route
Sound Planning the Evening: Echolocation as a Route Device
Without any sunlight, bats have developed a striking transformation to explore and find prey - echolocation. This organic sonar framework permits bats to transmit high-recurrence sound waves and decipher the reverberations that return, making a point by point hear-able guide of their environmental elements. Echolocation is an essential device that guides in route as well as assumes a vital part in chasing after bugs in obscurity.
This part dives into the mechanics of echolocation, investigating how bats produce and decipher sound waves to make a three-layered mental guide of their current circumstance. The variety of echolocation techniques among various bat species reflects variations to explicit natural specialties and hunting ways of behaving. From steady recurrence calls to recurrence regulated calls, the sonar ensemble of bat route is a demonstration of their tactile complexity.

Species-Explicit Echolocation: Fitting Sound for Endurance
Different bat species have advanced one of a kind echolocation systems that are finely tuned to their particular necessities and conditions. A few bats emanate calls at ultrasonic frequencies past the scope of human hearing, while others use lower frequencies that are discernible to us. The recurrence, power, and term of echolocation calls change, permitting bats to advance their sonar framework for the difficulties presented by their specific territories.

This part investigates the variety of echolocation systems among bats. From the complicated transformations of insectivorous bats to the social calls utilized by some organic product bats, the species-explicit subtleties of echolocation feature the adaptability of this tangible variation. Understanding how bats designer their echolocation capacities gives bits of knowledge into their biological jobs and developmental achievement.

4. Social Designs: Bats in Networks
Pilgrim Living: The Upsides of Collective Perches

Bats are frequently connected with common living, shaping enormous settlements that reach from a couple of people to millions. The upsides of mutual perching incorporate expanded security against hunters, sharing of data about food sources, and agreeable consideration of posterity. Some bat species display complex social designs that include progressive connections and agreeable ways of behaving.

This segment investigates the elements of bat states, from the mind boggling social designs of specific organic product bats to the thickly stuffed perches of bug eating bats. The shared living courses of action of bats exhibit the advantages of collaboration and sociality notwithstanding the difficulties presented by their nighttime ways of life. Understanding the complexities of bat networks gives a brief look into the helpful methodologies that have added to their transformative achievement.

Correspondence In obscurity: Vocalizations and Social Bonds

Correspondence is a fundamental part of social designs among bats, and vocalizations assume a urgent part in keeping up with social securities. Bats produce various vocalizations, going from calls that find perch mates to complex correspondence during romance and mating. Vocalizations are in many cases species-explicit, and a few bats have developed refined collections of calls to pass on data about food accessibility, region, and economic wellbeing.

This segment investigates the vocal correspondence of bats, underlining how vocalizations add to the attachment of bat networks. From the melodic romance tunes of some natural product bats to the quick fire echolocation calls of insectivorous bats, bat vocalizations are a rich and different part of their social way of behaving. Looking at the job of correspondence in bat networks gives bits of knowledge into the intricacy of their social designs.

5. Biological Specialty Inhabitance: Bats as Different Foragers
Insectivores in real life: Evening time Bug Control

Most of bat species are insectivores, and they assume a vital environmental part by filling in as nighttime bother regulators. Bug eating bats consume immense amounts of bugs, including farming vermin and sickness vectors.

Their capacity to unequivocally find and catch flying bugs in obscurity makes them priceless partners in keeping up with natural equilibrium and supporting human agrarian undertakings.

This segment investigates the scavenging procedures of insectivorous bats, from the nimble elevated quests for quick flying species to the drifting strategies of bats that gather bugs from vegetation. The variety of bat rummaging procedures reflects variations to various sorts of prey and territories. The natural specialty inhabitance of insectivorous bats highlights their importance in bug control and environment wellbeing.

Frugivores and Nectarivores: Seed Dispersers and Pollinators

Past insectivores, bats have enhanced into other dietary specialties, including frugivores (organic product eaters) and nectarivores (nectar feeders). Natural product bats assume a pivotal part in seed dispersal, supporting the recovery of woodlands and adding to the variety of plant species. Nectar-taking care of bats, with their particular transformations for tasting nectar, are significant pollinators for specific plant species.

This segment investigates the environmental commitments of natural product bats and nectar-taking care of bats. From the job of natural product bats in forming tropical environments to the fertilization administrations gave by nectarivorous bats to blossoming plants, the dietary variety of bats features their biological adaptability. Inspecting the connections among bats and the plants they associate with gives experiences into the interconnectedness of environments.

6. Dangers and Protection: Exploring an Influencing World
Human Effects: Natural surroundings Misfortune, Pesticides, and Environmental Change

In spite of their environmental significance, bats face various dangers from human exercises. Living space misfortune because of urbanization and deforestation lessens the accessibility of appropriate perching destinations and searching regions. The utilization of pesticides in farming can prompt the pollution of bat prey, influencing their wellbeing. Environmental change further intensifies these difficulties, adjusting the accessibility of food assets and disturbing the fragile natural equilibrium bats rely upon.

This part investigates the anthropogenic dangers confronting bat populaces. From the immediate effects of territory obliteration to the backhanded impacts of ecological changes, bats explore an influencing world molded by human exercises. Understanding the difficulties bats face is critical for creating successful preservation techniques to relieve the effects of human-actuated dangers.

White-Nose Condition: A Destructive Parasitic Infection

White-nose condition (WNS) is a staggering infection brought about by the growth Pseudogymnoascus destructans, which influences sleeping bats.

The parasite develops on the skin of bats, especially the wing layers and gag, disturbing hibernation examples and causing physiological pressure. WNS has prompted critical decreases in bat populaces, particularly in North America, and represents an extreme danger to a few bat animal varieties.

This part investigates the effects of white-nose condition on bat populaces. The development of WNS and its quick spread feature the weakness of bats to novel illnesses. Endeavors to comprehend and alleviate the impacts of this contagious infection are essential for the protection of bat species impacted by WNS.

4.1 Anatomy and physiology of bat flight

In the domain of flying well evolved creatures, bats stand as unmatched pilots, showing a dominance of the skies that opponents even the most achieved birds. The life structures and physiology of bat flight are a demonstration of the perplexing transformations that empower these well evolved creatures to explore the air with accuracy. This investigation dives into the exquisite ensemble of physical designs and physiological cycles that support the wonder of bat flight.

1. Winged Wonders: The Primary Outline of Bat Wings

The Patagium: An Adaptable Winged Film

At the center of bat flight lies the patagium, a flawlessly planned winged film that separates bats from different well evolved creatures. The patagium is an expansion of the skin between extended fingers, shaping a wing that is both sensitive and strong. This film permits bats to create lift, control their flight, and execute complicated moves with unparalleled deftness.

The patagium comes in different structures, reflecting transformations to various flight styles. In quick flying species, the wings might be long and limited, advancing for speed. Interestingly, bats adjusted for slow and floating flight have more extensive wings that upgrade mobility. This part investigates the underlying variety of bat wings, accentuating how the patagium fills in as the establishment for their airborne ability.

Lengthened Phalanges: The Fingerbones of Flight

Bats have lengthened fingerbones, especially the metacarpals and phalanges, which offer primary help for the patagium. The extending of these bones adds to the prolongation of the wing, taking into consideration a more noteworthy surface region and further developed lift. The fingers are additionally exceptionally adaptable, empowering bats to change wing shape and point during flight.

This part digs into the variations of bat fingerbones, investigating how the stretching and adaptability of these designs add to the biomechanics of flight.

From the main edge framed by the stretched digits to the following edge constrained by the membranous patagium, the mind boggling exchange of wing components permits bats to explore the skies with unmatched accuracy.

2. Muscle Power: The Motor Behind Bat Flight
Flight Muscles: Controlling Accuracy and Mobility
The capacity of bats to execute fast and exact flight moves is energized by a strong arrangement of flight muscles. These muscles are amassed in the chest and back, giving the power expected to move the wings during both the upstroke and downstroke. The intricacy of bat flight, from drifting to many-sided ethereal gymnastics, requires a finely tuned arrangement of flight muscles.

This segment investigates the course of action and capability of bat flight muscles, accentuating how the appropriation of bulk adds to the flexibility of their flight abilities. The coordination of muscles during wing development permits bats to accomplish the nimbleness vital for exploring through complex conditions and catching spry prey.

Metabolic Requests: The High-Energy Use of Flight
The requests of supported flight put a high metabolic weight on bats. The ceaseless fluttering of wings and the requirement for exact control during flight require a consistent stockpile of energy. Bats have developed metabolic transformations to satisfy these needs, including an exceptionally proficient respiratory framework and specific instruments for using fats.

This part digs into the metabolic transformations that help the high-energy consumption of bat flight. From the productivity of gas trade in the lungs to the use of put away fat stores during expanded flights, bats have developed physiological systems to support the high-impact requests of their airborne way of life.

3. Exploring In obscurity: Echolocation and Flight Coordination
Echolocation: A Sonic Toolbox for Route
In the nighttime world where bats rule, the capacity to explore and find prey in complete dimness is a basic part of their endurance. Echolocation, a natural sonar framework, permits bats to produce high-recurrence sound waves and decipher the reverberations that quickly return, making a point by point hear-able guide of their current circumstance.

This part investigates the coordination of echolocation with bat flight. The coordination of producing beats of sound, getting and handling reverberations, and changing flight directions in view of this data exhibit the multifaceted connection between tangible discernment and airborne route. The transformation of various echolocation techniques by different bat species mirrors their natural specialties and hunting ways of behaving.

Flight Coordination: The Dance of Accuracy

The marriage of echolocation with flight coordination is an expressive dance of accuracy, permitting bats to perform accomplishments that appear to be practically otherworldly. As bats explore through complex conditions, they change their flight ways in light of ongoing criticism from echolocation. The combination of tactile data with exact wing and body developments empowers bats to keep away from obstructions, catch tricky prey, and explore in complete murkiness.

This part dives into the complexities of flight coordination in bats. From the brief instant changes during pursuit to the coordinated moves expected for catching bugs mid-air, the synchronization of tactile contributions with engine reactions features the consistent reconciliation of bat life systems and physiology for aeronautical route.

4. Energy Effectiveness: The Biomechanics of Bat Flight

Streamlined features: Boosting Lift and Limiting Drag

The biomechanics of bat flight are a magnum opus of proficiency, permitting these warm blooded creatures to accomplish ideal lift and limit drag. The shape and adaptability of the patagium, combined with the many-sided developments of wing and tail, add to the streamlined rules that administer bat flight. Understanding the biomechanics of flight gives experiences into how bats accomplish energy-productive flying headway.

This segment investigates the streamlined variations of bat wings, stressing the manners by which wing morphology and development add to the advancement of lift and the decrease of drag. From the collapsing of wings during the upstroke to the use of vortices for expanded lift, bats have developed biomechanical arrangements that permit them to preserve energy during flight.

Muscle Productivity: The Force of Transformation

Productive energy usage is vital for the supported trip of bats, particularly given the high metabolic requests of their way of life. Bats have developed muscle variations that improve the productivity of their flight. The capacity to specifically draw in unambiguous muscles during various periods of wing development, combined with the energy-saving systems of floating and taking off, adds to the general energy effectiveness of bat flight.

This part dives into the muscle transformations that permit bats to accomplish effective and supported flight. From the tweaking of muscle compressions to the usage of updrafts and air flows for floating, the biomechanical systems of bats grandstand the developmental advancements that have made them especially adjusted to the aeronautical domain.

5. Maturing and Life span: The Effect of Trip on Bat Life expectancy
Life span and Flight: An Inquisitive Connection
In the normal world, the connection among flight and life expectancy is a captivating
part of bat science. In spite of the lively requests of supported flight, bats frequently
show longer life expectancies contrasted with non-flying vertebrates of comparable size.
The explanations for this connection among's flight and life span are not completely
perceived, yet a few speculations recommend that the metabolic transformations
expected for flight might give life span benefits.
This part investigates the charming association between bat flight and life expectancy.
From the expected enemy of maturing impacts of raised metabolic rates to the job of trip
in staying away from ground-based hunters, the variables adding to the drawn out life
expectancies of bats add a layer of intricacy to the comprehension of the transformative
benefits related with flight.

Senescence and Transformations: Exploring the Difficulties of Maturing
As bats age, they, similar to all creatures, face the difficulties of senescence — the
steady disintegration of natural capabilities over the long run. The fact that warrants
further examination makes in any case, the effect of maturing on bat flight and generally
wellness a subject. The variations that bats might show to adapt to the difficulties of
maturing, especially with regards to flight, give experiences into the transaction among
life span and the requests of an ethereal way of life.
This part digs into the transformations and difficulties related with maturing in bats.
From expected changes in flight examples to the job of social designs and public living
in supporting more established people, the investigation of maturing with regards to bat
flight reveals insight into the powerful collaborations between physiology, conduct, and
the progression of time.

4.2   Echolocation as a navigation tool in the dark
In the front of haziness, where the shortfall of light clouds the world, certain animals
have advanced remarkable transformations to explore their environmental factors.
Among them, bats have culminated a method known as echolocation, a natural sonar
framework that permits them to see and decipher their current circumstance through
sound waves. This investigation dives into the unpredictable universe of echolocation,
unwinding the systems, flexibility, and natural meaning of this amazing route apparatus
in obscurity.

1. The Essentials of Echolocation: Sonic Waves in the Evening
Creating Sound: A Vocal Ensemble

At the core of echolocation is the discharge of sound waves by the bat. Bats are fit for delivering a different cluster of calls, going from high-recurrence ultrasonic heartbeats to perceptible snaps. These calls act as the sonic signs that bats use to test their environmental factors. The age of sound is an essential part of echolocation, and different bat species have developed explicit call qualities custom fitted to their biological requirements.

This segment investigates the course of sound creation in echolocating bats. From the vocal life structures that considers call age to the regulation of call recurrence and power, the emanation of sound signs is a painstakingly coordinated ensemble that characterizes the viability of echolocation as a route instrument.

Getting Reverberations: The Arrival of Sonic Data

When the radiated sound waves experience objects in the climate, they return quickly as reverberations. Bats have profoundly touchy ears equipped for identifying and deciphering these reverberations with exceptional accuracy. The ears of bats are finely tuned to get reverberations across a wide scope of frequencies, permitting them to build definite mental guides of their environmental elements in light of the timing and qualities of reverberation returns.

This part digs into the hear-able ability of bats, underlining the transformations in their ear structures that work with the gathering of reverberations. From the shape and size of the ears to the particular designs that guide in confining sound, the unpredictable life systems of bat ears mirrors the transformative refinement of their echolocation capacities.

2. Species-Explicit Echolocation: Fitting Sound for Endurance
The Variety of Bat Calls: Adjusting to Natural Specialties

One of the striking parts of echolocation is the variety of calls delivered by various bat species. The variety in call recurrence, term, and example isn't arbitrary yet is unpredictably connected to the biological specialties and hunting procedures of every species. A few bats discharge calls at ultrasonic frequencies past the scope of human hearing, while others utilize perceptible calls.

This part investigates the species-explicit subtleties of bat echolocation calls. From the steady recurrence calls of specific bats to the recurrence balanced calls of others, the variety in call qualities reflects variations to explicit environments, prey types, and searching ways of behaving. The capacity of bats to tailor their calls for ideal execution in their separate surroundings features the adaptability of echolocation as a versatile apparatus.

Hunting Techniques: Adjusting Echolocation to Prey Catch

Past basically exploring their current circumstance, bats use echolocation as an exact instrument for hunting and catching prey. Different bat species have developed explicit hunting techniques in view of the attributes of their echolocation calls. For instance, a few bats radiate fast, consistent recurrence calls appropriate for recognizing flying bugs, while others use recurrence regulated calls for more nitty gritty objective separation. This part digs into the connection among echolocation and hunting procedures in bats. The transformations in call structure, including beat span, recurrence reach, and reiteration rate, feature the refined manners by which bats streamline their echolocation capacities for fruitful prey catch. The transformative weapons contest among bats and their prey has driven the refinement of echolocation as an instrument for successful hunting.

3. The Craft of Target Limitation: Planning the Dull
Deciphering Reverberations: Developing Mental Guides

The way to effective echolocation lies in the capacity of bats to decipher the reverberations getting back from their environmental factors. As sound waves experience objects, they make repeats that convey data about the distance, size, shape, and even surface of those items. Bats have developed the ability to quickly handle this sonic data, permitting them to build definite mental guides of their current circumstance continuously.

This segment investigates the course of target confinement in echolocating bats. The timing and power of reverberations give urgent data about the area and qualities of items, empowering bats to explore through complex conditions, stay away from snags, and find prey with amazing accuracy. The mental capacities related with echolocation feature the reconciliation of tangible discernment and engine reactions in the bats' elevated collection.

The Doppler Impact: Detecting Movement through Sound

Notwithstanding static items, echolocation permits bats to distinguish and decipher the movement of their environmental elements. The Doppler impact, a peculiarity connected with changes in recurrence brought about by the movement of a sound source or beneficiary, assumes a vital part in this part of echolocation. Bats use the Doppler impact to detect the development of prey, conspecifics, or even hindrances in their flight way.

This part digs into how the Doppler impact adds to the powerful capacities of echolocation. From following the unpredictable trip of bugs to keeping away from impacts during fast moves, the capacity of bats to detect movement through changes in reverberation recurrence adds a layer of complexity to their route tool stash.

4. Echolocation and Ecological Variations: Exploring Different Natural surroundings
Acoustic Specialties: Fitting Echolocation to Territories
Various territories present one of a kind difficulties and potential open doors for echolocating bats. Bats have advanced explicit acoustic transformations to explore different conditions, going from open spaces to jumbled vegetation. The idea of "acoustic specialties" depicts how different bat species have adjusted their echolocation calls to streamline execution in unambiguous living spaces.
This segment investigates the idea of acoustic specialties in bat biology. From the open space calls of bats that rummage in the airspace above water bodies to the limited transmission capacity calls of bats that explore thick vegetation, the transformations in echolocation mirror the natural specialties that bats possess. Understanding these variations gives bits of knowledge into the assorted manners by which bats use echolocation for endurance in various living spaces.

Worldly and Spatial Adaptability: Changing Echolocation to Conditions
Echolocation is definitely not an inflexible framework however one that bats can change powerfully founded on the states of their current circumstance. Bats show transient and spatial adaptability in their echolocation calls, changing the recurrence, length, and example of brings in light of variables, for example, foundation commotion, mess, and the nearness of articles.
This part dives into how bats adjust their echolocation progressively to suit natural circumstances. From expanding call power in uproarious conditions to restricting the pillar width in jumbled spaces, the adaptability of echolocation permits bats to keep up with effective route across a scope of territories. The powerful changes in echolocation exhibit the versatility of this tactile apparatus.

4.3   The ecological importance of bats as pollinators and insect controllers

Bats, frequently covered in legends and misinterpretations, assume pivotal natural parts that stretch out a long ways past the domain of the evening. Two jobs, specifically, stand apart as demonstration of their importance - fertilization and bug control. This investigation dives into the biological significance of bats as the two pollinators and regulators of bug populaces, disentangling the complicated connections that bats produce with plants and the environment.

1. The Quiet Landscapers: Bats as Pollinators
The Fertilization Expressive dance: Bats and Blossoming Plants

In the peaceful hours of the evening, when numerous pollinators rest, bats become the dominant focal point as nighttime grounds-keepers.

The mutualistic connection among bats and blooming plants is a fragile expressive dance of coevolution, where each accomplice benefits. Bats, looking for nectar as a food source, incidentally move dust starting with one bloom then onto the next, working with the conceptive outcome of plants.

This segment investigates the job of bats as pollinators and the extraordinary variations that have developed in the two bats and plants to encourage this multifaceted organization. From the physical highlights of bat-adjusted blossoms to the tactile transformations of nectar-taking care of bats, the fertilization expressive dance unfurls as a demonstration of the interconnectedness of life in the nighttime biological system.

Bat-Adjusted Blossoms: An Ensemble of Shapes and Fragrances

To draw in bat pollinators, certain blossoms have advanced unmistakable qualities that line up with the tangible inclinations of bats. These transformations frequently incorporate huge, open, and durable blossoms, delivering bountiful measures of nectar. Moreover, many bat-pollinated blossoms serious areas of strength for radiate around evening time, upgrading their perceptibility by bats in obscurity.

This part digs into the captivating variations of bat-adjusted blossoms. From the remarkable shapes and sizes of botanical designs to the synthetic signals that guide bats to nectar sources, the variety of bat-pollinated plants mirrors the accuracy of coevolution. The orchestra of shapes and fragrances in bat-adjusted blossoms features the perplexing manners by which plants have developed to draw in and control their nighttime pollinators.

2. Gatekeepers of Biodiversity: Bats as Seed Dispersers
Natural product Bats: Planting the Seeds of Variety

Notwithstanding their job as pollinators, natural product bats, or frugivorous bats, assume a significant part in seed dispersal. By consuming products of the soil venturing out to various areas, these bats assist with scattering seeds, adding to the variety and recovery of plant species. The viability of bat-interceded seed dispersal turns out to be especially crucial in living spaces where other dispersal specialists might be restricted.

This segment investigates the environmental significance of natural product bats as seed dispersers. From the dietary inclinations of various natural product bat species to the distances over which seeds can be scattered, the job of bats in forming plant networks highlights their importance in keeping up with biodiversity. The cooperation between organic product bats and plants in the dispersal and foundation of seeds epitomizes the interconnectedness of species in biological systems.

Biological Administrations: Bats as Landscapers of the Evening

The biological administrations given by bats reach out past their nearby connections with plants.
 As natural product bats scatter seeds, they add to the foundation and endurance of plant populaces. This, thus, influences the construction and organization of biological systems, affecting the wealth of plant species and the variety of related fauna. This part digs into the more extensive environmental ramifications of bat-intervened seed dispersal. From the rebuilding of corrupted scenes to the production of different environments that help a bunch of animal categories, bats arise as quiet nursery workers of the evening, forming biological systems through their job in seed dispersal. The environmental administrations given by bats reverberation across biological systems, underscoring their significance in keeping up with the fragile equilibrium of biodiversity.

3. Evening time Nuisance Control: Bats as Bug Regulators
The Flying Chase: Bats as Bosses of the Night Sky
Bats are famous for their uncommon abilities to hunt, especially with regards to catching bugs on the wing. Many bat species are insectivores, and their insatiable craving for nighttime bugs has acquired them the title of nature's irritation regulators. The environmental significance of bats in controlling bug populaces is a dynamic and fundamental part of their job in biological systems.
This segment investigates the ruthless ability of bats and their job as regular bug regulators. From the transformations in bat life systems and echolocation for successful hunting to the assorted rummaging techniques utilized by various bat species, the evening chase unfurls as a basic biological help given by bats. The proficiency of bats in controlling bug populaces adds to the security of environments and has broad ramifications for horticulture and human prosperity.

Monetary Advantages: Bats in Farming and Then some
The effect of bats on bug populaces conveys critical monetary advantages. In rural scenes, bats assist with controlling harvest harming vermin, lessening the requirement for substance pesticides. The worth of bats in bother control stretches out to ranger service, where they add to shielding trees from destructive bugs. Past farming, bats assume an essential part in keeping up with the wellbeing of environments by controlling sickness conveying bugs.
This part investigates the monetary and environmental advantages of bats as regular vermin regulators. From the decrease of harvest harm to the relief of sicknesses spread by bugs, bats proposition important administrations that unmistakably affect human prosperity and the strength of indigenous habitats. Perceiving and valuing the commitments of bats in bug control is fundamental for feasible and harmless to the ecosystem bother the board rehearses.

4. Protection Difficulties: Dangers to Bat Populaces
Confronting the Evening: Difficulties to Bat Endurance

Regardless of their natural significance, bat populaces overall face various dangers that imperil their endurance. Environment misfortune, contamination, environmental change, and the spread of illnesses, for example, white-nose condition present huge difficulties to bat populaces. The preservation of bats isn't just fundamental for safeguarding biodiversity yet additionally for keeping up with the biological administrations they give. This segment digs into the preservation challenges that bats experience. From the immediate effects of territory obliteration to the backhanded impacts of ecological changes, bats explore an influencing world formed by human exercises. Understanding the difficulties bats face is pivotal for creating compelling protection techniques to moderate the effects of human-prompted dangers.

White-Nose Disorder: An Approaching Danger

White-nose disorder (WNS) is an overwhelming parasitic illness that influences sleeping bats, especially in North America. The parasite, Pseudogymnoascus destructans, upsets hibernation designs, making physiological pressure and driving huge decreases in bat populaces. WNS represents a serious danger to a few bat animal categories and highlights the weakness of bats to novel sicknesses.

This segment investigates the effects of white-nose disorder on bat populaces. The rise of WNS and its fast spread feature the dire requirement for preservation endeavors to address the sickness and safeguard weak bat species. Understanding the intricacies of sickness elements in bat populaces is fundamental for creating systems to relieve the effects of WNS and different dangers.

Chapter 5
Humans Take Flight

The fantasy of flight has been a determined and captivating craving all through mankind's set of experiences. From the legendary stories of Icarus to the portrayals in Leonardo da Vinci's note pads, the yearning to take off through the skies has filled the human creative mind. This investigation dives into the surprising excursion of people taking off, from the earliest yearnings to the mechanical victories that have characterized flight.

1. The Beginning of Dreams: Early Dreams of Flight
Fantasies and Legends: Icarus and Then some
The craving to fly is well established in human folklore, with stories of winged creatures and divine flight saturating societies across the world. The narrative of Icarus, who designed wings from plumes and wax, fills in as a useful example, featuring both the charm and the perils related with the quest for flight. Legendary stories, while fantastical, mirror the natural human interest with the opportunity and viewpoint that flight guarantees.

This segment investigates the fantasies and legends that have formed mankind's initial dreams of flight. From old Greek folklore to stories from old China and India, the social and emblematic meaning of trip in human narrating makes way for the developing journey to transform the fantasy of trip into an unmistakable reality.

Leonardo da Vinci: Portrayals in the Journal
In the Renaissance time, the splendid psyche of Leonardo da Vinci mulled over the mechanics of flight. His definite draws and plans for flying machines, including ornithopters and lightweight planes, laid the foundation for grasping optimal design and the standards of lift. Albeit a considerable lot of da Vinci's plans were never fabricated or tried, his visionary commitments denoted a crucial second in the progress from dreams of trip to the logical investigation of streamlined features.

This segment digs into Leonardo da Vinci's commitments to the early comprehension of flight. From his physical investigations of birds to his multifaceted plans for flying machines, da Vinci's note pads uncover a sharp interest in the conceivable outcomes of human flight and the logical rules that oversee it.

2. Inflatables and the Time of Edification
Montgolfier Siblings: The Development of Tourist Balloons

The eighteenth century saw a progressive jump as humanity continued looking for trip
with the development of sight-seeing balloons. Joseph and Étienne Montgolfier, siblings
from France, spearheaded the advancement of these airborne wonders. In 1783, their
sight-seeing balloon, decorated with a paper envelope, climbed into the skies,
conveying the expectations and goals of the people who really hoped for leaving the
World's surface.

This part investigates the cutting edge second when sight-seeing balloons turned into
the primary human-conveying vehicles to accomplish controlled flight. The Montgolfier
siblings' accomplishment denoted a defining moment throughout the entire existence of
flying, showing the way that people could to be sure vanquish the skies and witness the
world from a completely new viewpoint.

3. The Trailblazers of Fueled Flight: Wright Siblings and Then some
Wright Siblings: Opposing Gravity at Kitty Falcon

The stupendous jump from swelling to fueled flight occurred in the mid twentieth 100
years with the Wright siblings, Orville and Wilbur. In December 1903, on the desolate
ridges of Kitty Falcon, North Carolina, the Wright Flyer took off, denoting the first
controlled, fueled, and supported trip in a heavier-than-air machine. The
accomplishment of the Wright siblings proclaimed the beginning of present day flying
and changed the fantasy of trip into a reality.

This part investigates the essential second at Kitty Falcon and the careful designing
endeavors that prompted the outcome of the Wright Flyer. From the imaginative plan of
the airplane to the standards of optimal design applied by the Wright siblings, the
excursion from dreams to the acknowledgment of controlled flight is divulged.

Brilliant Time of Flying: Crossing Seas and Establishing Standards

The mid twentieth century saw a quick development in flying innovation, prompting
trying accomplishments and record-breaking flights. Pilots, for example, Charles
Lindbergh caught the world's creative mind by finishing the primary performance
relentless overseas trip in 1927. The period became known as the Brilliant Time of
Flying, set apart by achievements that pushed the limits of what was viewed as
conceivable in the domain of flight.

This segment investigates the Brilliant Time of Flying and the accomplishments that
characterized this period. From Lindbergh's memorable trip to Amelia Earhart's
spearheading endeavors in transoceanic and transoceanic avionics, the boldness and
vision of early pilots established the groundwork for the worldwide development of air
travel.

4. The Fly Age and Business Aeronautics
Fly Impetus: Breaking the Sound wall

The mid-twentieth century saw one more groundbreaking jump in aeronautics innovation with the improvement of stream motors. The sound wall, when thought about an outlandish obstruction, was broken by Hurl Yeager in 1947 as he directed the Ringer X-1 rocket-controlled airplane. Stream drive reformed air travel, empowering quicker and more effective flights that made ready for the business aeronautics industry.

This part investigates the approach of stream drive and its effect on avionics. From military applications to the presentation of jetliners for business travel, the Fly Age introduced a period of exceptional speed and openness, bringing individuals closer and making air travel an ordinary encounter.

Business Avionics Takes Off

The post-The Second Great War time saw the quick development of business flying, changing air travel from an extravagance for the special minority to a method of transportation open to the majority. The Boeing 707, presented in 1958, is much of the time viewed as the main financially fruitful jetliner, denoting the start of another period where air travel turned into an imperative piece of worldwide network.

This part investigates the development of business flying and the mechanical progressions that made air travel more open. From the improvement of enormous planes like the Boeing 747 to the foundation of worldwide air travel organizations, business avionics turned into a fundamental part of current transportation, interfacing individuals and societies across the globe.

5. Space Investigation: Arriving at Past Earth's Air
The Space Race: Yuri Gagarin and the Apollo Missions

The fantasy of flight reached out past the World's air during the twentieth hundred years with the approach of room investigation. The Space Race, filled by the opposition between the US and the Soviet Association, arrived at a notable achievement in 1961 when Yuri Gagarin turned into the principal human to circle the Earth. The Apollo missions, drove by NASA, further extended the limits of human investigation, coming full circle in the notable moon arriving in 1969.

This segment investigates the Space Race and the accomplishments that moved people into space. From Gagarin's notable circle to the stupendous Apollo 11 mission that saw Neil Armstrong and Buzz Aldrin stroll on the lunar surface, space investigation denoted another part in mankind's excursion past the bounds of our planet.

Transports, Stations, and Then some: The Time of Shuttle

Following the Apollo missions, the space transport time started, presenting reusable shuttle that worked with more regular and savvy admittance to space.

The development of room stations, including the Global Space Station (ISS), gave stages to long haul human presence in space. The investigation of Mars, automated missions to far off planets, and the advancement of private space organizations further extended humankind's venture into the universe.

This segment investigates the advancement of room investigation past the Apollo period. From the Space Transport program to the development and activity of room stations, the narrative of people wandering into space keeps on unfurling with headways in innovation, worldwide cooperation, and the endeavors of both government organizations and confidential undertakings.

6. Future Boondocks: Supersonic Travel and Then some
Supersonic Dreams: Breaking the Sound wall Once more

As of late, there has been recharged interest in supersonic travel, with organizations investigating the chance of bringing back business supersonic flights. The commitment of decreased travel times and the charm of flying quicker than the speed of sound have reignited the fantasy of supersonic traveler travel.

This segment investigates the new improvements in supersonic flying and the difficulties related with bringing back business supersonic flights. From progressions in optimal design to the likely ecological worries, the quest for supersonic travel addresses a contemporary boondocks in flying that expands upon the accomplishments of the past.

Past Earth: Mars Colonization and Interstellar Dreams

Looking forward, the fantasy of flight stretches out past Earth to the possibility of human colonization of Mars and the investigation of interstellar space. Visionaries like Elon Musk imagine a future where people lay out a super durable presence on Mars, while logical endeavors investigate the potential outcomes of interstellar travel to far off star frameworks.

This segment investigates the advanced outskirts of human flight, from the likely colonization of Mars to the speculative domains of interstellar travel. While these thoughts stay in the domain of hypothesis, they address the continuous human mission to push the limits of what is attainable in the immense region of room.

5.1   History and evolution of human flight

The craving to vanquish the skies, to break the natural bonds and take off among the mists, has been a persevering through dream all through mankind's set of experiences. From the earliest fantasies of winged creatures to the cutting edge wonders of room investigation, the excursion of human flight is a demonstration of the unyielding soul of investigation and development. This investigation follows the rich history and advancement of human flight, from the legendary goals of antiquated societies to the mechanical victories that characterize contemporary aviation attempts.

1. Fantasy and Creative mind: Wings of Antiquated Dreams
Antiquated Folklores: Icarus and Then some

The underlying foundations of humankind's interest with flight can be tracked down in the legends of old societies. In Greek folklore, the story of Icarus fills in as a preventative tale about the risks of arriving at excessively near the sun with wings formed from quills and wax. The imagery of Icarus mirrors the synchronous appeal and danger related with the quest for trip in the human creative mind.

This part investigates the legendary beginnings of human flight, digging into stories from antiquated Greece, India, China, and then some. The repetitive topic of winged creatures and divine beings crossing the sky mirrors the widespread longing for flight and the mysterious association between the earthbound and heavenly domains in the aggregate human cognizance.

Leonardo da Vinci: Representations in the Renaissance Sky

While antiquated legends powered the fantasy of flight, it was during the Renaissance that human interest started to converge with logical request. Leonardo da Vinci, frequently viewed as the quintessential Renaissance polymath, left behind itemized draws and plans for flying machines in his scratch pad. However these visionary ideas were not understood in his time, da Vinci's physical investigations of birds and mind boggling plans for ornithopters and lightweight flyers laid the foundation for figuring out the standards of streamlined features.

This segment investigates Leonardo da Vinci's commitments to the early comprehension of flight. His portrayals, going from flying machines propelled by birds to parachute plans, exhibit a combination of creative vision and logical request that set up for the possible development of human departure from creative mind to the real world.

2. Inflatables and the Victory of Lightness
Montgolfier Siblings: The Ascent of Sight-seeing Balloons

The eighteenth century saw a noteworthy progress from fantasy and draws to substantial examinations with flight. The Montgolfier siblings, Joseph and Étienne, impacted the world forever in 1783 with the primary monitored trip in a sight-seeing balloon. Their inflatable, embellished with a paper envelope and filled by the warming of air, rose into the skies, denoting the commencement of controlled human flight.

This part investigates the improvement of tourist balloons and the notable trip of the Montgolfier siblings. The creation of inflatables addressed a change in outlook, showing the way that people could for sure rise into the skies and witness the world according to a raised viewpoint. Expanding turned into an image of human creativity and the victory of lightness over the gravitational draw of the Earth.

3. Controlled Flight: The Wright Siblings and Then some
Wright Siblings: Vanquishing Kitty Falcon

The amazing jump from inflatables to fueled, controlled flight occurred in the mid twentieth 100 years with the Wright siblings, Orville and Wilbur. In 1903, at the desolate rises of Kitty Bird of prey, North Carolina, the Wright Flyer took off, denoting the principal supported, controlled trip in a heavier-than-air machine. The 12-second, 120-foot venture changed the fantasy of trip into a reality and introduced the period of current flying.

This part investigates the noteworthy accomplishment at Kitty Falcon and the careful designing endeavors that prompted the outcome of the Wright Flyer. From the inventive plan of the airplane to the utilization of standards of streamlined features, the Wright siblings' achievement established the groundwork for the advancement of human flight and the blossoming field of flying.

Brilliant Period of Flying: Trailblazers and Records

Following the Wright siblings' memorable flight, the mid twentieth century saw a fast development in flying innovation. The Brilliant Time of Aeronautics, traversing the 1920s and 1930s, was set apart by trying accomplishments and record-breaking flights. Pilots, for example, Charles Lindbergh caught the world's creative mind with the principal solo relentless transoceanic trip in 1927, and Amelia Earhart pushed the limits of significant distance flying.

This part investigates the Brilliant Time of Flight and the accomplishments that characterized this period. From Lindbergh's memorable trip to Earhart's spearheading endeavors in transoceanic and transoceanic flight, the boldness and vision of early pilots laid the preparation for the worldwide extension of air travel.

4. Stream Impetus and the Fly Age
Breaking the Sound wall: Hurl Yeager's Achievement

The mid-twentieth century acquired one more groundbreaking jump flying innovation with the improvement of stream motors. Throw Yeager, a U.S. Flying corps pilot, accomplished a notable achievement in 1947 by breaking the sound wall in the Chime X-1 rocket-fueled airplane. The approach of fly drive upset air travel, empowering quicker and more productive flights that undeniable the start of the Stream Age.

This part investigates the presentation of stream drive and its effect on avionics. From military applications to the development of jetliners for business travel, the Fly Age introduced a period of remarkable speed and availability, making air travel more proficient and far and wide.

Business Flying Takes Off
The post-The Second Great War period saw the fast development of business flying, changing air travel from an extravagance for the special minority to a method of transportation open to the majority. The presentation of business jetliners, for example, the Boeing 707 out of 1958, denoted a huge achievement in making air travel more proficient and worldwide open.
This part investigates the development of business flight and the innovative progressions that made air travel more open. From the advancement of enormous planes like the Boeing 747 to the foundation of worldwide air travel organizations, business flying turned into an indispensable piece of current transportation, associating individuals and societies across the globe.

5. Space Investigation: Trying the impossible
The Space Race: Yuri Gagarin and Apollo Missions
The fantasy of flight stretched out past Earth's air during the twentieth hundred years with the appearance of room investigation. The Space Race, energized by the opposition between the US and the Soviet Association, arrived at a notable achievement in 1961 when Yuri Gagarin turned into the principal human to circle the Earth. The Apollo missions, drove by NASA, further extended the limits of human investigation, coming full circle in the notable moon arriving in 1969.
This part investigates the Space Race and the accomplishments that moved people into space. From Gagarin's noteworthy circle to the stupendous Apollo 11 mission that saw Neil Armstrong and Buzz Aldrin stroll on the lunar surface, space investigation denoted another section in humankind's excursion past the limits of our planet.

Space Transports and Worldwide Joint effort
Following the Apollo missions, the time of room transports started, presenting reusable space apparatus that worked with more successive and savvy admittance to space. The development of room stations, including the Global Space Station (ISS), gave stages to long haul human presence in space. The joint effort of different countries in the investigation of room exhibited the potential for global collaboration in logical undertakings.
This part investigates the development of room investigation past the Apollo period. From the Space Transport program to the development and activity of room stations, the account of people wandering into space keeps on unfurling with headways in innovation, global cooperation, and the endeavors of both government organizations and confidential undertakings.

6. Contemporary Boondocks: Supersonic Travel and Then some
Supersonic Dreams: Breaking the Sound wall Once more

As of late, there has been a resurgence of interest in supersonic travel, with organizations investigating the chance of bringing back business supersonic flights. The commitment of diminished travel times and the appeal of flying quicker than the speed of sound have reignited the fantasy of supersonic traveler travel.

This part investigates the new improvements in supersonic avionics and the difficulties related with bringing back business supersonic flights. From headways in optimal design to possible ecological worries, the quest for supersonic travel addresses a contemporary wilderness in flight that expands upon the accomplishments of the past.

Past Earth: Mars Colonization and Interstellar Dreams

Looking forward, the fantasy of flight stretches out past Earth to the possibility of human colonization of Mars and the investigation of interstellar space. Visionaries like Elon Musk imagine a future where people lay out a long-lasting presence on Mars, while logical endeavors investigate the potential outcomes of interstellar travel to far off star frameworks.

This part investigates the advanced outskirts of human flight, from the possible colonization of Mars to the speculative domains of interstellar travel. While these thoughts stay in the domain of hypothesis, they address the continuous human mission to push the limits of what is feasible in the huge field of room.

5.2 Technological advancements in aviation

The historical backdrop of flight is unpredictably woven with an embroidery of mechanical progressions that have moved the business from the simple plans of the Wright siblings to the state of the art developments of the cutting edge period. This investigation digs into the groundbreaking excursion of flying innovation, following its development from the beginning of propellers to the ongoing outskirts of hypersonic speeds.

1. Propellers and Cylinder Motors: The Beginning of Controlled Flight
Wright Siblings' Propeller-driven Flight

The commencement of controlled trip by the Wright siblings in 1903 denoted the start of another time, where flying innovation changed from the domains of creative mind to unmistakable reality. The Wright Flyer, fueled by a cylinder motor and propellers, exhibited the standards of controlled, supported flight. This early airplane laid the basis for resulting improvements in avionics innovation.

This part investigates the spearheading utilization of propellers and cylinder motors in the Wright siblings' airplane.

From the plan of the airplane's wings and the complexities of propeller-driven impetus to the designing difficulties of accomplishing lift and solidness, the early long periods of avionics were characterized by steady progressions that made ready for additional refined advancements.

2. The Second Great War and the Introduction of Military Flying
Warrior Airplane and Dogfights

The episode of The Second Great War catalyzed fast progressions in flight innovation, driven by the requests of military clash. Warrior airplane became essential parts of ethereal fighting, and the time saw the introduction of dogfights — extraordinary flying fights between contradicting pilots. Mechanical advancements zeroed in on further developing airplane execution, improving capability, and presenting developments, for example, synchronized automatic rifles.

This part investigates the mechanical progressions prodded by the tactical requests of The Second Great War. From the presentation of military aircraft like the Fokker Dr.I and the Sopwith Camel to the development of elevated strategies, the conflict turned into a cauldron for testing and refining flying innovations, making way for the interwar period.

3. Between the Conflicts: Business Aeronautics Takes Off
Metal Development and Smoothing out

The period between the conflicts saw the development of aeronautics innovation and the rise of business flight. Metal development, especially the utilization of aluminum, supplanted the prior wooden designs, improving the strength and sturdiness of airplane. Furthermore, smoothing out turned into a key plan standard, enhancing streamlined features to lessen drag and further develop eco-friendliness.

This part investigates the change from military to business aeronautics and the mechanical advancements that characterized the interwar period. The improvement of metal-outlined airplane like the Boeing 247 and the acquaintance of smoothed out plans contributed with the development of business air travel, making it more effective and open.

4. The Second Great War: Fly Impetus and Radar Unrest
Fly Impetus: The Messerschmitt Me 262

The Second Great War achieved a change in outlook in flying innovation with the presentation of stream drive. The Messerschmitt Me 262, a German stream contender, turned into the world's most memorable functional fly fueled airplane. Fly motors offered fundamentally higher rates and heights contrasted with propeller-driven airplane, reforming the abilities of military aeronautics.

This segment investigates the effect of fly drive on flight innovation during The Second Great War. From the Me 262 to the English Gloster Meteor and the American P-80 Falling star, stream fueled airplane reshaped the elements of ethereal battle and established the groundwork for the post-war time of business fly travel.

Radar Innovation: Eyes overhead
Simultaneously, radar innovation arose as a unique advantage in flying. Radar gave a method for identifying and following airplane over significant distances, upgrading situational mindfulness and empowering more viable air safeguard. The combination of radar into military flight assumed a critical part in forming the result of fights and impacting post-war improvements in aviation authority and route.
This segment dives into the progressive effect of radar innovation on flying during The Second Great War. From early ground-based radar frameworks to airborne radar on airplane like the English Beaufighter, radar turned into a basic part of flight, adding to both military and regular citizen applications.

5. The Stream Age and Business Flight
Business Jetliners: The Boeing 707
The post-The Second Great War period saw the commercialization of fly travel, introducing the Fly Age. The Boeing 707, presented in 1958, denoted a huge achievement as the main economically effective jetliner. Stream impetus changed business flying, offering remarkable speed and proficiency, diminishing travel times, and making air head out more open to a worldwide crowd.
This segment investigates the approach of business jetliners and their effect on flying innovation. The Boeing 707, trailed by other famous airplanes like the Douglas DC-8 and the Convair 880, opened up additional opportunities for significant distance air make a trip and added to the globalization of economies and societies.

6. High level Flying and Computerization
Fly-by-Wire Frameworks and Glass Cockpits
The late twentieth century saw an unrest in flying and cockpit innovation. Fly-by-wire frameworks, supplanting conventional mechanical control frameworks with electronic connection points, became standard in current airplane. Glass cockpits, highlighting computerized shows and electronic flight instrumentation frameworks (EFIS), supplanted customary simple measures, giving pilots more instinctive and data rich points of interaction.
This segment investigates the progressions in flying and cockpit innovation that described the last option part of the twentieth hundred years.

The Airbus A320, with its spearheading fly-by-wire framework, and the Boeing 777, including an exhaustive glass cockpit, represent the shift towards more modern and computerized flight control frameworks.

7. Supersonic Travel and Difficulties
Concorde: The Supersonic Trailblazer
The mission for quicker air venture out prompted the improvement of supersonic business airplane, with the Concorde remaining as an image of this desire. The Concorde, a joint endeavor among English and French aviation ventures, entered administration in 1976 and could journey at speeds over two times the speed of sound. In any case, difficulties like sonic blasts, high working expenses, and natural worries restricted the broad reception of supersonic travel.

This segment investigates the mechanical accomplishments and difficulties related with supersonic business travel. The Concorde's one of a kind plan and designing, alongside the obstacles it confronted, feature the intricacies of accomplishing rapid air travel.

8. Arising Outskirts: Hypersonic Rates and Electric Impetus
Hypersonic Flight: X-15 and X-43
As flying entered the 21st hundred years, the center moved to significantly higher rates with the investigation of hypersonic flight. The X-15, a rocket-controlled airplane, set speed standards during the 1960s, arriving at speeds over Mach 6. All the more as of late, the X-43, an automated hypersonic airplane, accomplished speeds surpassing Mach 9, exhibiting the potential for hypersonic flight.

This part investigates the headways in hypersonic innovation and the difficulties related with accomplishing supported and controlled trip at such high velocities. Hypersonic flight addresses an outskirts that holds guarantee for quicker and more productive air travel, as well as applications in military and space investigation.

Electric Drive and Reasonable Aeronautics
In the journey for more reasonable flying, electric drive has arisen as a critical area of development. Electric airplane, controlled by batteries or crossover electric frameworks, intend to diminish natural effects and reliance on petroleum derivatives. Organizations are effectively creating electric drive innovations for different airplane sizes, from little metropolitan air portability vehicles to territorial and, surprisingly, enormous business planes.

This part dives into the mechanical improvements in electric impetus and their capability to reshape the fate of flying. The shift towards feasible aeronautics lines up with more extensive endeavors to diminish fossil fuel byproducts and address ecological worries inside the flight business.

5.3   The intersection of art and science in human-made flight

Human-made flight is an enthralling orchestra where the apparently different domains of workmanship and science meet, delivering harmonies that reverberation across the skies. This investigation digs into the rich transaction among workmanship and science in avionics, unwinding the complex movement of imagination and designing that has characterized the development of flight.

1. Planning Dreams: Feel in Airplane Plan
Class in the Skies: Structure and Capability

Airplane plan, at its embodiment, is an artistic expression that weds feel with usefulness. From the smooth lines of supersonic planes to the lofty wingspan of enormous carriers, the visual allure of airplane reflects both designing ability and a sign of approval for imaginative sensibilities. Planners endeavor not exclusively to upgrade optimal design yet in addition to make airplane that are outwardly striking, exemplifying a feeling of effortlessness and reason.

This part investigates the style of airplane configuration, accentuating the harmony among structure and capability. The Concorde, with its famous thin fuselage and delta wings, remains as a demonstration of the reconciliation of style and designing in making a supersonic show-stopper. The advancement of wing shapes, fuselage plans, and the utilization of materials like carbon composites all add to the creative articulation implanted in the rawness of flight.

2. The Craft of Advancement: Conceptualizing Future Flight
Advanced Ideas: Obscuring Limits

The convergence of craftsmanship and science in flying stretches out past the present, wandering into the domain of advanced ideas that challenge our view of what flight can be. Idea airplane, frequently displayed in flight shows and plan rivalries, push the limits of creative mind and designing. These visionary manifestations, like flying wings, vertical departure and landing (VTOL) vehicles, and individual air taxis, address the blend of imaginative vision and mechanical development.

This segment investigates the creativity intrinsic in conceptualizing future flight. Visionary originators and specialists team up to make airplane that resist show as well as exemplify a feeling of style and development. Whether propelled essentially or driven by a craving for maintainability, these reasonable airplanes embody the boundless potential outcomes when craftsmanship and science join to rethink the skies.

3. Visual Narrating: Airplane Uniform and Marking
Flying Materials: The Specialty of Airplane Attire

Past the actual type of airplane, the outsides act as powerful materials for visual narrating.

Airplane uniform, including paint plans, logos, and marking, is a strong medium through which carriers express their personality and lay out a visual association with travelers. The imaginativeness engaged with making special and conspicuous uniforms changes planes into flying show-stoppers, each recounting the aircraft's way of life, history, or goals.

This part digs into the specialty of airplane attire and marking. The notorious plans of aircrafts like English Aviation routes, with its ageless Association Jack tail blade, or the dynamic examples of minimal expense transporters, add to the visual woven artwork of flying. Past feel, uniform assumes a part in forming the traveler experience and making a feeling of association among explorers and the carriers they pick.

4. Photography and Aeronautics: Catching the Substance of Flight
Wings of Viewpoint: The Photographic artist's Focal point

Photography plays had a crucial impact in catching the substance and excellence of flight. Aeronautics picture takers, equipped with cameras and a natural enthusiasm for flight, freeze minutes in time that convey the unique energy, effortlessness, and force of airplane. From aerial photography that catches planes in trip to ground shots that underline the sheer size of aeronautics framework, these pictures rise above the specialized into the domain of workmanship.

This segment investigates the harmonious connection among flying and photography. From the perspective, picture takers become narrators, encapsulating aeronautics occasions, airshows, and ordinary minutes at air terminals. Their work reports the advancement of airplane as well as hoists the enthusiasm for trip to an artistic expression, permitting lovers and the overall population to partake in the miracle of aeronautics.

5. Persuasive Craftsmanship: Avionics in Expressive arts and Writing
Winged Dream: Flying in Expressive arts

Flying has been a dream for craftsmen across different mediums, tracking down articulation in canvases, figures, and different types of expressive arts. The charm of flight, the imagery of wings, and the juxtaposition of machines against the setting of the sky have motivated endless specialists to make reminiscent works that catch the quintessence of human-made flight. From the avionics themed works of art of Norman Rockwell to the figures of notable airplane, these fine arts add to the social tradition of aeronautics.

This segment investigates the effect of aeronautics on expressive arts and the manners by which specialists decipher the magnificence and meaning of flight. The otherworldly idea of flying furnishes craftsmen with a material whereupon to investigate subjects of opportunity, investigation, and the human soul's mission for the skies.

Scholarly Wings: Avionics in Writing

Flight has likewise tracked down its direction into the composed word, where creators weave stories that rise above the specialized parts of avionics to investigate its significant effect on the human experience. From the trying undertakings of pilots to the figurative utilization of trip in writing, flying fills in as a scholarly theme that reflects subjects of mental fortitude, investigation, and the vast potential outcomes of the human soul.

This segment digs into the portrayal of aeronautics in writing, from exemplary works like Antoine de Holy person Exupéry's "The Little Ruler" to contemporary books that investigate the intricacies of life overhead. The marriage of flying and writing makes stories that resound with perusers, offering an exceptional point of view on the difficulties and wins of the individuals who take to the skies.

6. Mechanical Materials: Flying in Computerized Expressions
Computerized Masterfulness: Activity and Augmented Reality

In the computerized age, flying has turned into a material for craftsmen working in liveliness and augmented reality (VR). Advanced imaginativeness considers the formation of vivid encounters that transport watchers into the core of flying, offering dynamic points of view and intelligent narrating. Whether through vivified short movies that catch the enchantment of flight or VR recreations that permit clients to encounter cockpit sees, these computerized manifestations push the limits of imaginative articulation in aeronautics.

This part investigates the convergence of avionics and advanced expressions, exhibiting how innovation empowers craftsmen to push the limits of imagination. Energized shorts like "Paperman," which joins conventional hand-drawn movement with state of the art innovation, or VR encounters that mimic the vibe of flight add to another period of creative investigation in aeronautics.

Chapter 6
The Ballet of Migration

In the tremendous material of the normal world, movement arises as quite possibly of the most striking and amicable expressive dance, a mind boggling dance organized by endless species across the globe. This investigation jumps into the universe of relocation, disentangling the natural, biological, and conduct subtleties that shape this fabulous ensemble of development. From the famous excursions of birds to the noteworthy relocations of marine life and earthly miracles, the expressive dance of movement unfurls as a demonstration of the flexibility and versatility imbued in the texture of life.

1. The Orchestra Starts: Grasping Relocation
Characterizing Relocation: A General Peculiarity

Relocation, in the domain of the collective of animals, is a peculiarity profoundly imbued in the methods for surviving of various species. Characterized as the occasional development starting with one locale then onto the next, relocation fills different needs, including tracking down better assets, getting away from unforgiving ecological circumstances, or replicating in ideal areas. From bugs and birds to vertebrates and fish, the idea of relocation rises above ordered limits, uncovering itself as a widespread procedure for variation.

This part digs into the central parts of relocation, investigating its fluctuated structures and purposes across various species. The movement examples of wildebeest in the Serengeti, the legendary excursion of ruler butterflies, and the overseas relocations of marine life embody the variety and intricacy of this normal peculiarity. The expressive dance of relocation, with its shifted movement, starts to unfurl on a worldwide stage.

2. Avian Tastefulness: The Ethereal Expressive dance of Bird Movement
Wings Across Mainlands: Amazing Avian Excursions

Bird relocation stands apart as perhaps of the most entrancing and proven and factual exhibition in the normal world. From the Icy tern's surprising excursion covering large number of miles between its favorable places in the Icy and the Antarctic to the notable yearly movements of waterfowl like ducks and geese, the avian artful dance of relocation paints the skies with a material of wings.

This segment investigates the airborne tastefulness of bird movement, digging into the science behind the peculiarity. Navigational components, the job of divine prompts, and the amazing accomplishments of perseverance showed by transient birds uncover the complexities of avian movement.

From the air V-arrangements of Canada geese to the performance trips of gooney birds, the avian artful dance becomes the dominant focal point in the excellent orchestra of movement.

3. Earthly Odyssey: The Land-based Relocations
Hooves and Paws Moving: Land-based Movements

While birds overwhelm the aeronautical domain of relocation, earthly scenes take the stand concerning the cadenced developments of vertebrates across tremendous distances. Land-based movements exhibit the versatility and flexibility of species like wildebeest, caribou, and zebras. These relocations frequently range whole landmasses, driven by the mission for food, water, or the need to arrive at favorable places.
This part digs into the earthly odyssey of land-based movements, investigating the surprising excursions of notable species. The Serengeti's extraordinary relocation, where wildebeest and zebras cross the fields looking for crisp munching, and the caribou groups of the Icy, covering huge distances to find appropriate calving grounds, embody the earthly expressive dance of movement. The recurring pattern of hooves and paws across scenes become a demonstration of the repeating rhythms of life.

4. Marine Wonders: The Maritime Artful dance of Movement
Exploring the Blue: Marine Movements

The seas, immense and baffling, have the absolute most remarkable movements on earth. From the great excursions of marine warm blooded animals like whales and dolphins to the staggering odysseys of ocean turtles and fish, the maritime artful dance of movement unfurls underneath the surface. These movements frequently length large number of miles, interfacing different marine biological systems and assuming a critical part yet to be determined of marine life.
This segment dives into the profundities of marine relocations, revealing the secret developments underneath the waves. The extraordinary relocations of humpback whales, incorporating great many miles among taking care of and favorable places, and the legendary journey of leatherback ocean turtles crossing whole sea bowls to settle on unambiguous sea shores, represent the wonders of marine movement. The seas, overflowing with life and development, become a phase for an artful dance that traverses huge seascapes.

5. The Undetectable Excursions: Bug Relocations
Little Wings, Great Excursions: Bug Relocations

Bugs, notwithstanding their minute size, participate in probably the most amazing movements on The planet. From the sensitive vacillating of butterflies to the decided trips of grasshoppers, bug relocations cross landmasses and add to biological cycles like fertilization and irritation control.

These imperceptible excursions, frequently unseen by human onlookers, feature the basic job bugs play in keeping up with the wellbeing and equilibrium of environments. This part investigates the little yet amazing movements of bugs, divulging the complexities of their excursions. The ruler butterfly's amazing relocation from North America to focal Mexico and the synchronized developments of grasshopper swarms that can traverse whole locales epitomize the variety and meaning of bug movements. The expressive dance of relocation stretches out its scope to the littlest occupants of the regular world.

6. The Rhythms of Life: Favorable places and Then some
The Circle of Life: Rearing, Movement, and Return

Relocation is a vital piece of the existence cycle for some species, framing a perplexing and interconnected trap of environmental connections. The excursion from favorable places to taking care of regions and back is a repeating expressive dance that guarantees the continuation of life. The determination of reasonable favorable places, the route of hazardous courses, and the re-visitation of natural territories all add to the multifaceted rhythms of life.

This segment investigates the total life pattern of transitory species, revealing insight into the interconnectedness of various living spaces. The Icy tern's settling grounds in the Icy, the taking care of regions along relocation courses, and the re-visitation of these basic territories for the cutting edge embody the repetitive idea of movement. The artful dance of relocation, with its ages old movement, is a fundamental component in the propagation of biodiversity.

7. Natural Difficulties: The Battle for Endurance
Impediments Along the Way: Human Effect and Environmental Change

While relocation is a demonstration of the versatility of species, it isn't without its difficulties. Human exercises, like territory annihilation, contamination, and urbanization, present critical dangers to transient courses and visit locales. Environmental change further fuels these difficulties, adjusting the planning of relocation, influencing food accessibility, and prompting shifts in biological systems.

This part tends to the natural difficulties looked by transient species and the fragile equilibrium they should keep up with to get by. The effect of human exercises on transient courses, represented by the predicament of the North Atlantic right whale confronting transport strikes and snare in fishing gear, highlights the weakness of these glorious excursions. The expressive dance of relocation faces an undeniably mind boggling stage, requesting preservation endeavors to protect the uprightness of transitory pathways.

8. Preservation Movement: Safeguarding the Artful dance of Relocation
Saving the Dance: Protection Endeavors and Examples of overcoming adversity
Despite mounting difficulties, preservation endeavors assume a urgent part in protecting
the artful dance of relocation. Safeguarded regions, global joint efforts, and local area
based drives add to defending the living spaces and movement courses basic for the
endurance of transient species. Examples of overcoming adversity, for example, the
recuperation of the California condor and the protection endeavors for the beating
crane, embody the positive effect of purposeful preservation activities.
This segment investigates the preservation movement that looks to safeguard and
support the expressive dance of relocation. The foundation of untamed life halls, the
assignment of basic territories, and the contribution of nearby networks in protection
endeavors address ventures toward guaranteeing the proceeded with display of
relocation. Through these drives, people can assume a part in safeguarding the
immortal dance of transient species.

6.1   Overview of migration patterns in flying species

Movement, a peculiarity unpredictably woven into the texture of the regular world, takes
on a hypnotizing aspect when seen in flying species. Birds, bugs, and, surprisingly, bats
set out on flying odysseys, covering tremendous distances across landmasses and
seas. This investigation gives an extensive outline of relocation designs in flying
species, disentangling the secrets of their heavenward excursions. From the
navigational wonders of transitory birds to the sensitive trip of butterflies and the
nighttime journeys of bats, the airborne expressive dance of movement divulges itself
as a demonstration of the noteworthy transformations that empower these species to
cross the skies.

1. Navigational Miracles: The Elevated Expressive dance of Transient Birds
Divine Compass and Attractive Guides
Transient birds, maybe the most famous of flying travelers, explore the skies with
dumbfounding accuracy. Their capacity to cross a huge number of miles among
reproducing and wintering grounds depends on a complicated exchange of inborn
senses and ecological signals. Birds use a divine compass, adjusting their flight ways to
the place of the sun and stars. Moreover, they utilize the World's attractive field as a
navigational guide, permitting them to keep an internal compass in any event, during
cloudy circumstances.
This segment dives into the navigational miracles of transitory birds, investigating the
instruments that guide their trips across mainlands. The mind boggling dance of sandhill
cranes over North America, the long distance race excursions of Cold terns between
polar limits, and the cooperative V-developments of Canada geese embody the variety
of navigational procedures utilized by avian transients.

2. Rulers Moving: Butterfly Relocation and Streamlined Wonders
Winged Miracles on the Wing

Butterflies, fragile and apparently ethereal, attempt noteworthy transitory excursions that challenge our impression of these winged miracles. The ruler butterfly, specifically, catches consideration with its cross-country movement traversing North America. The excursion of rulers includes numerous ages, with people flying a huge number of miles to arrive at their wintering grounds in Mexico. In spite of their delicate appearance, butterflies feature streamlined wonders in their flight, using air ebbs and flows and thermals to cover significant stretches.

This segment investigates the airborne expressive dance of butterfly movement, zeroing in on the extraordinary transformations that empower these bugs to explore across scenes. The many-sided life pattern of ruler butterflies, their capacity to involve ecological signs for route, and the job of progressive ages in finishing the movement cycle highlight the intricacy of butterfly relocations.

3. Bats in the Night Sky: Nighttime Pilots of Relocation
Quiet Wings in the Haziness

While birds and bugs rule the daytime skies during movement, bats arise as nighttime pilots, quietly exploring the night looking for ideal searching and favorable places. Bat relocation, however less noticeable to human eyewitnesses, is a peculiarity that grandstands the exceptional transformations of these warm blooded creatures. Bats utilize echolocation, transmitting high-recurrence sounds and deciphering the reverberations, to explore and find prey during their nighttime flights.

This segment reveals insight into the extraordinary parts of bat movement, underlining the transformations that make them bosses of the night sky. The significant distance trips of aged bats, the cooperative way of behaving of Brazilian free-followed bats in shaping enormous settlements, and the environmental meaning of bat movements in keeping up with bug populaces feature the essential job these warm blooded creatures play in nighttime biological systems.

4. The Imperceptible Odyssey: Bug Movement Examples
Minuscule Flyers, Fabulous Excursions

Bugs, in spite of their minor size, participate in the absolute most exceptional movement designs on The planet. From dragonflies and grasshoppers to moths and scarabs, different bug species cover amazing distances during their relocations. These excursions are much of the time fundamental for their endurance, adding to environmental cycles, for example, fertilization, bug control, and hereditary variety. This segment disentangles the undetectable odyssey of bug movement designs, exhibiting the variety of flying species that set out on stupendous excursions.

The synchronized trips of grasshopper swarms, the awe-inspiring movements of painted woman butterflies, and the fragile elevated expressive dance of dragonflies highlight the natural significance of bug relocations and their effect on different biological systems.

5. Occasional Rhythms: Grasping the Planning of Relocation
Precision Flights: Opportune Takeoffs and Appearances

Movement is definitely not a heedless event yet follows exact occasional rhythms directed by changes in temperature, light, and food accessibility. Understanding the planning of movement is vital for flying species as they set out on their excursions. Occasional signs, for example, photoperiod (day length), trigger physiological changes that immediate people to plan for movement. The capacity to synchronize flight and appearance with good natural circumstances is fundamental for the outcome of these excursions.

This part investigates the occasional rhythms that administer the planning of movement in flying species. The synchronized takeoff of barnacle geese from Cold favorable places, the essential timing of dragonfly relocations in light of atmospheric conditions, and the planned mass developments of ruler butterflies throughout the fall embody the mind boggling timing systems that drive transient way of behaving.

6. Natural Difficulties: Dangers Along the Flyway
Hazards in the Skies: Human Effect and Environmental Change

While relocation is a demonstration of the flexibility of flying species, it isn't without its difficulties. Human exercises, including territory obliteration, contamination, and crashes with man-made structures, present huge dangers to transient courses and visit locales. Environmental change further intensifies these difficulties, adjusting the accessibility of food and influencing the planning of relocation.

This part tends to the natural difficulties looked by flying transients along their flyways. The effect of human exercises on transitory courses, showed by the dangers looked by taking off birds during their movement across mainlands, highlights the weakness of these excursions. The expressive dance of movement faces an undeniably complicated stage, requesting preservation endeavors to safeguard the trustworthiness of transient pathways.

7. Preservation Movement: Shielding Ethereal Relocations
Safeguarding the Ensemble: Protection Endeavors and Examples of overcoming adversity

Despite mounting difficulties, preservation endeavors assume an essential part in safeguarding the artful dance of relocation in flying species.

Safeguarded regions, worldwide coordinated efforts, and local area based drives add to defending the environments and movement courses basic for the endurance of transitory birds, bugs, and bats. Examples of overcoming adversity, for example, the recuperation of the eastern populace of outshining cranes and the protection endeavors for the jeopardized lesser long-nosed bat, represent the positive effect of purposeful preservation activities.

This segment investigates the preservation movement that tries to secure and support the expressive dance of relocation in flying species. The foundation of transient bird safe-havens, the assignment of basic territories, and the contribution of neighborhood networks in preservation endeavors address ventures toward guaranteeing the proceeded with exhibition of movement. Through these drives, people can assume a part in protecting the immortal dance of elevated transients.

6.2   The role of navigation and environmental cues in long-distance flight

Significant distance flight is a peculiarity that rises above the limits of landmasses, seas, and environments. Flying species, from transient birds to bugs and bats, set out on ventures covering huge number of miles, depending on a modern transaction of route and ecological prompts. This investigation dives into the multifaceted systems that guide these avian, bug, and mammalian voyagers, disentangling the job of route and ecological signs in the remarkable domain of significant distance flight.

1. Heavenly Map making: Avian Route in the Skies
The Heavenly Embroidery as an Aide

For transient birds, the divine territory fills in as a navigational embroidery, directing them across immense distances with noteworthy accuracy. The sun, stars, and, surprisingly, the World's attractive field become heavenly waypoints, supporting birds in deciding their heading and keeping a consistent course. The capacity to peruse these signs is imbued in their hereditary code, considering transformations that empower them to explore during both constantly.

This part investigates the divine map making used by transitory birds. The sun, going about as a dependable compass, gives a steady reference point during light hours. Nighttime travelers, like larks, utilize the stars for route, displaying an astounding skill to perceive explicit heavenly bodies and change their flight as needs be. The mind boggling dance of route inside the heavenly circle unfurls as a fundamental part of significant distance flight.

2. Earth's Attractive Tune: Avian Magnetoreception
Directed by Attractive Murmurs

Notwithstanding divine prompts, transitory birds have a wonderful capacity known as magnetoreception, permitting them to distinguish the World's attractive field. This sense of direction fills in as a significant apparatus for route, particularly during shady or cloudy circumstances when divine signals might be darkened. The exact components behind avian magnetoreception are as yet a subject of logical request, yet scientists accept it includes particular cells containing magnetite, an attractive mineral.

This part digs into the baffling universe of avian magnetoreception. The usage of the World's attractive field as a navigational guide empowers birds to keep up with course in any event, when viewable signals are restricted. The perplexing transaction among heavenly and attractive direction frameworks grandstands the versatile wonders that have advanced to work with significant distance trip in avian transients.

3. Bugs in Flight: Exploring by the Sun and Then some
Little Guides, Huge Excursions

Bugs, notwithstanding their humble size, take part in significant distance flights that range mainlands and assume pivotal parts in environmental cycles. Their route depends on a mix of viewable signals, especially the sun, and intrinsic direction systems. Bugs, like butterflies and dragonflies, use the sun's situation to keep an internal compass during their relocations.

This segment enlightens the universe of bug route, underscoring the dependence on obvious prompts. The sun, going about as a noticeable signal, guides bugs across scenes, empowering them to cover noteworthy distances. The novel transformations in their compound eyes and multifaceted standards of conduct add to the effectiveness of their route, exhibiting the different procedures utilized by bugs in their significant distance flights.

4. Bats in the Night Sky: Reverberations and Heavenly Route
Nighttime Ability In obscurity

Bats, the nighttime pilots of the mammalian world, explore the night skies with a blend of echolocation and heavenly prompts. While some bat species are known for their significant distance relocations, others take part in daily rummaging flights covering broad regions. Echolocation, the emanation of high-recurrence sounds and the translation of returning reverberations, permits bats to explore and find prey. Heavenly signs, like the moon and stars, likewise assume a part in directing their nighttime processes.

This part reveals the nighttime ability of bats in significant distance flight. Echolocation fills in as a unique device for route, permitting bats to explore through complex conditions and find prey in complete murkiness.

Heavenly signs, including the moon's situation and star designs, give extra reference focuses to their excursions. The variation to a nighttime way of life features the flexibility of bats in overcoming the difficulties of significant distance flight.

5. Ecological Milestones and Geology: Visual Route in Flight
Tourist spots and Landscape as Guideposts
Past divine and attractive prompts, flying species frequently depend on visual acknowledgment of natural milestones and geographical highlights to explore across scenes. For transient birds, particular elements, for example, shorelines, mountain reaches, and waterways act as visual guideposts, supporting direction and course choice. This visual route turns out to be especially critical during sunlight hours when heavenly signals are best.
This part investigates the dependence on natural tourist spots and geology in significant distance flight. The essential utilization of topographical highlights, for example, the Appalachian Mountains filling in as a navigational hall for warblers, represents the significance of obvious signals in directing transitory excursions. The joining of visual route with different components highlights the multi-layered approach that flying species utilize to explore across assorted landscapes.

6. Ecological Effects on Flight Examples: Climate and Wind Direction
Outfitting Environmental Powers
Ecological circumstances, particularly atmospheric conditions and wind flows, altogether impact the flight examples of transient species. Flying against headwinds consumes more energy, provoking species to change their flight heights and courses to bridle great climatic circumstances. Understanding and adjusting to weather conditions become fundamental abilities for effective significant distance flight, guaranteeing energy proficiency and limiting the difficulties presented by unfavorable circumstances. This segment dives into the effect of climate and wind on the flight techniques of transient species. The usage of tailwinds for energy protection, the aversion of unfriendly climate frameworks, and the variation of flight elevations in view of air conditions exhibit the powerful reactions of flying species to natural impacts. The coordination of climate mindfulness turns into a necessary part of the navigational toolbox for significant distance transients.

7. Social Transmission and Learning: Navigational Information Passed Down
Shrewdness of the Accomplished
In certain species, particularly birds, there is proof of social transmission and learning in the domain of route. Adolescent people frequently gain transitory courses and navigational signs from experienced grown-ups, taking into consideration the transmission of navigational information across ages.

This social part of route adds a layer of intricacy to the natural systems, exhibiting the meaning of learned ways of behaving in effective significant distance flight.

This part investigates the job of social transmission in navigational information. The mentorship among experienced and adolescent people, as seen in species like the outshining crane, adds to the conservation of transitory customs. The mix of natural navigational impulses and learned ways of behaving improves the versatility and outcome of flying species in exploring the difficulties of significant distance flight.

6.3   Conservation challenges and solutions for migratory species

The expressive dance of movement, an immortal ensemble performed by flying species across the globe, faces a variety of preservation challenges that undermine the uprightness of their excursions. As transient species cross mainlands, seas, and scenes, they experience hazards along the flyway, going from environment obliteration and contamination to environmental change and human-prompted impediments. This investigation dives into the preservation challenges looked by transitory species and divulges inventive arrangements that intend to safeguard these wonderful excursions, guaranteeing the progression of the airborne expressive dance that has spellbound humankind for ages.

1. Environment Misfortune and Fracture: A Contracting Stage
The Disappearing Scenes

One of the essential difficulties looked by transitory species is the misfortune and discontinuity of their basic living spaces. Urbanization, agrarian extension, and modern improvement bring about the annihilation of reproducing, taking care of, and visit locales. The contracting of these fundamental scenes upsets the normal rhythms of movement, driving species to explore through an inexorably divided and threatening climate.

This segment investigates the effect of environment misfortune and discontinuity on transient species. The situation of shorebirds losing essential visit locales along their movement courses, the fracture of backwoods influencing warbler favorable places, and the provokes looked by marine travelers because of seaside advancement embody the dire need to address natural surroundings misfortune. Preservation arrangements should zero in on safeguarding and reestablishing these imperative territories to give transitory species the fundamental stages for their spectacular processes.

2. Contamination: The Poisonous Inclinations
From Land to Sky: A Contaminated Excursion

Contamination, in its different structures, represents an unavoidable danger to transitory species all through their excursions.

Compound poisons, plastic waste, and oil slicks defile air, land, and water, influencing the environments whereupon transitory species depend. The outcomes of contamination stretch out past quick openness, prompting long haul influences on the wellbeing and endurance of flying transients.

This segment dives into the treacherous impacts of contamination on transitory species. The difficulties looked via seabirds ingesting plastic flotsam and jetsam, the defilement of wetlands and water bodies influencing waterfowl, and the airborne toxins influencing the respiratory frameworks of transitory birds highlight the criticalness of tending to contamination along relocation courses. Protection endeavors should focus on the decrease of contamination and the rebuilding of impacted biological systems to shield the strength of transient species.

3. Environmental Change: Moving Standards
The Erratic Undeniable trends

Environmental change arises as an impressive danger to the sensitive equilibrium of transient excursions. Modified temperature designs, changes in precipitation, and changing occasional signs upset the synchronicity between the planning of movement and the accessibility of assets. Transitory species, finely sensitive to explicit ecological circumstances, face moves in adjusting to the quickly evolving environment, prompting jumbles in timing and expanded weakness.

This segment analyzes the effect of environmental change on transient species. The moving rearing and taking care of grounds of Icy terns because of warming temperatures, the modified timing of blossoming influencing pollinator relocations, and the provokes looked by marine transients because of sea fermentation feature the intricate transaction between environmental change and movement. Preservation methodologies should consolidate environment versatile ways to deal with relieve the effects of a changing environment on transient species.

4. Human-Prompted Deterrents: Impacts in the Skies
Man-Made Risks Along Movement Courses

As transitory species explore their aeronautical courses, they experience a rising number of human-incited deterrents. Crashes with designs, for example, structures, correspondence pinnacles, and wind turbines present critical dangers to birds and bats in flight. Light contamination, brought about by unnecessary counterfeit lighting, can bewilder nighttime travelers, prompting crashes and fatigue. The development of transportation organizations, including streets and electrical cables, further pieces living spaces and builds the gamble of impacts.

This segment investigates the dangers presented by human-actuated hindrances along movement courses.

The difficulties looked by birds slamming into tall designs during their excursions, the effect of light contamination on the route of nighttime travelers, and the dangers related with electrical cables crossing movement hallways highlight the requirement for moderation measures. Preservation arrangements should address these impediments to limit the human-prompted dangers to flying transients.

5. Overharvesting and Double-dealing: Upsetting the Regular Equilibrium
The Kind of Overexploitation

Certain transient species face dangers from overharvesting and double-dealing, as they become focuses for business purposes or customary practices. Overfishing in marine conditions influences the accessibility of prey for seabirds and marine vertebrates. The unlawful exchange of transient birds and their eggs represents an immediate danger to populaces previously confronting difficulties during their excursions. Economical administration practices and global participation are vital for address the overharvesting of transient species.

This segment dives into the difficulties presented by overharvesting and double-dealing along movement courses. The effect of overfishing on the food wellsprings of transitory marine species, the unlawful exchange of transient birds, and the dangers looked by transitory butterflies because of living space annihilation for business purposes feature the direness of tending to overexploitation. Preservation endeavors should focus on manageable practices and implement guidelines to control the adverse impacts of human exercises on transitory species.

6. Protection Arrangements: A Brought together Methodology
Protecting the Expressive dance of Relocation

Tending to the protection challenges looked by transient species requires a far reaching and brought together methodology that rises above boundaries and disciplines. Protection arrangements should be multi-layered, integrating territory safeguarding, contamination decrease, environment versatility, and economical administration rehearses. Global cooperation, local area commitment, and the mix of conventional information are significant parts of effective preservation endeavors.

This segment frames key preservation answers for protect the artful dance of movement:

Environment Safeguarding and Rebuilding: Focus on the assurance and reclamation of basic living spaces, including rearing, taking care of, and visit locales, to furnish transient species with the essential stages for their excursions. Lay out and keep up with natural life hallways to interface divided scenes.

Contamination Decrease: Carry out measures to lessen contamination along relocation courses, including the legitimate removal of plastic waste, the guideline of compound poisons, and the relief of oil slicks. Support people group drove drives for squander the board and ecological stewardship.

Environment Flexibility: Create and carry out environment tough methodologies that record for the effects of environmental change on transitory species. This incorporates the production of safeguarded regions, living space the executives, and examination on versatile ways of behaving because of changing natural circumstances.

Moderation of Human-Initiated Deterrents: Carry out measures to alleviate the effect of human-actuated snags along movement courses. This incorporates the essential position of wind turbines, the adjustment of building plans to decrease impact gambles, and the guideline of light contamination in nighttime environments.

Maintainable Administration Practices: Implement feasible administration rehearses for fisheries and other regular assets to forestall overharvesting and abuse. Draw in nearby networks in feasible asset use, advancing elective vocations that help both human necessities and the preservation of transient species.

Global Joint effort: Encourage worldwide participation and coordination among nations along relocation courses. Create and execute arrangements, arrangements, and activity intends to address transboundary protection challenges. Support drives like the Show on Transient Species (CMS) and the Ramsar Show on Wetlands.

Local area Commitment: Include neighborhood networks in protection endeavors, perceiving the significance of conventional information and practices. Bring issues to light about the natural meaning of transient species and their environments, encouraging a feeling of stewardship among networks living along relocation courses.

Exploration and Checking: Lead examination to improve comprehension of transitory species' ways of behaving, nature, and reaction to ecological changes. Carry out observing projects to follow populace patterns, movement courses, and the adequacy of protection measures.

Schooling and Support: Advance training and backing drives to raise public mindfulness about the significance of transitory species and the protection challenges they face. Draw in with policymakers, organizations, and people in general to advocate for strategies that help the assurance of transient courses and living spaces.

Chapter 7
Flight in the Future

The domain of flight, a demonstration of human inventiveness and the developmental wonders of nature, is ready to enter another time — one characterized by state of the art advances, creative plans, and a reconsidering of the skies. This investigation dives into the fate of flight, unwinding the conceivable outcomes that look for us as we explore the boondocks of aeronautics, space investigation, and the proceeded with variation of flying organic entities. From progressive airplane plans to space the travel industry, supportable drive frameworks, and the joining of man-made brainpower, the fate of flight vows to be an enamoring venture into strange skies.

1. The Development of Airplane Plan: From Ideas to The real world Cutting edge Flying Machines

The fate of flight holds invigorating possibilities for the advancement of airplane configuration, testing customary ideas and pushing the limits of streamlined features. Ideas, for example, mixed wing bodies, electric vertical departure and landing (eVTOL) vehicles, and measured air vehicles are ready to change air travel. These developments guarantee expanded effectiveness, diminished ecological effect, and upgraded flexibility in exploring metropolitan scenes.

This segment investigates the advancement of airplane plan from here on out. The advancement of mixed wing body airplane, which coordinate the fuselage and wings for further developed optimal design and eco-friendliness, addresses a change in outlook in flying. Moreover, eVTOL vehicles, described by electric impetus and vertical departure capacities, offer additional opportunities for metropolitan portability and brief distance travel. The approach of measured air vehicles, with adjustable designs for different missions, features the versatility of future flying machines.

2. Metropolitan Air Portability: Changing City Skies From Gridlocks to Air Roadways

The idea of metropolitan air portability (UAM) imagines a future where the skies above urban communities are flawlessly incorporated into the transportation organization. Electric air cabs, drones, and independent ethereal vehicles are set to change metropolitan driving, reducing ground blockage and giving proficient, on-request elevated transportation. The improvement of UAM framework, including vertiports and air traffic the executives frameworks, is fundamental for understanding the maximum capacity of metropolitan airspace.

This part digs into the groundbreaking capability of UAM in molding the eventual fate of flight. Electric air taxis, intended for brief distance metropolitan travel, offer a brief look into a future where suburbanites can sidestep ground blockage and arrive at their objections with exceptional speed. Independent flying vehicles, directed by cutting edge route frameworks and computerized reasoning, add to the vision of a dynamic and interconnected metropolitan airspace. The foundation of vertiports, much the same as flying centers, and complex air traffic the executives frameworks is significant for guaranteeing the protected and effective activity of UAM.

3. Electric Drive: Reclassifying Reasonable Flight
Humming into the Green Skies

The eventual fate of flight is complicatedly connected to the quest for supportability, and electric drive arises as a key empowering influence in this journey. Electric airplane, driven by battery-fueled motors, guarantee diminished fossil fuel byproducts and calmer activities. Progresses in battery innovation, including the improvement of high-energy-thickness batteries, are pivotal for broadening the reach and abilities of electric avionics. This segment investigates the job of electric impetus in reclassifying the manageability of flight. Electric airplane, going from little electric mentors to territorial carriers, are ready to become fundamental parts of future armadas. The journey for high-energy-thickness batteries, fit for putting away and conveying a lot of electrical energy, is a basic part of electric flight improvement. The potential for electric drive to change short-pull flights, decrease clamor contamination, and add to the decarbonization of the aeronautics business is at the front line of the maintainable flight development.

4. Supersonic and Hypersonic Travel: Past the Speed of Sound
Sonic Blasts and Climatic Skimming

The eventual fate of flight holds the commitment of supersonic and hypersonic travel, where business airplane can navigate the globe at extraordinary rates. Supersonic carriers, for example, the arrival of the Concorde or the improvement of new-age supersonic planes, offer decreased travel times and a re-visitation of quicker than-sound flight. Hypersonic vehicles, fit for speeds more noteworthy than Mach 5, open up opportunities for quick intercontinental travel and admittance to space.
This part investigates the resurgence of supersonic travel and the development of hypersonic abilities. The likely return of supersonic business flights, set apart by diminished sonic blasts and progressions in streamlined features, presents a thrilling wilderness in avionics. Hypersonic vehicles, impelled by scramjet motors and fit for going at outrageous rates, hold guarantee for upsetting admittance to space and empowering quick worldwide transportation.

The difficulties of dealing with the natural effect and guaranteeing wellbeing at such high rates highlight the requirement for cautious turn of events and guideline in the domain of supersonic and hypersonic flight.

5. Space The travel industry: Connecting the Divine Bay
From Terrestrial to Astrotourist

The fate of flight reaches out past Earth's environment, welcoming regular people to become astrotourists and experience the marvels of room. Space the travel industry organizations are effectively creating suborbital flights that give brief excursions to the edge of room, permitting people to encounter weightlessness and witness the curve of the Earth. The commercialization of room travel opens up additional opportunities for private people to become spacefarers.

This part dives into the expanding field of room the travel industry and its extraordinary effect on the eventual fate of flight. Organizations, for example, Blue Beginning and Virgin Cosmic are spearheading suborbital spaceflights, offering regular people a sample of the spacefaring experience. The improvement of reusable rocket advancements and the foundation of business spaceports are key components in making space the travel industry more available. The crossing point of mechanical advancement, administrative systems, and the yearnings of people to wander past Earth's air characterizes the direction of room the travel industry in the years to come.

6. Man-made brainpower in Avionics: From Co-Pilot to Independence
The Mental Skies

Man-made consciousness (computer based intelligence) is ready to assume a vital part in molding the eventual fate of flight, from upgrading airplane frameworks to empowering independent tasks. Artificial intelligence driven aeronautics frameworks, versatile flight control, and keen dynamic abilities guarantee expanded security, effectiveness, and dependability in flying. The movement toward independent flight, where simulated intelligence expects a focal job in route and direction, addresses a change in outlook in the human-machine relationship.

This segment investigates the reconciliation of man-made consciousness into the flight scene. Artificial intelligence driven aeronautics, furnished with cutting edge sensors and AI calculations, improve the capacities of airplane frameworks, giving ongoing information examination and prescient upkeep. The progress toward independent flight, set apart by artificial intelligence fueled direction and route, brings up issues about wellbeing, administrative structures, and the moral contemplations of giving up control to canny frameworks. The coordinated effort between human pilots and simulated intelligence, mixing the qualities of both, characterizes the mental skies representing things to come.

7. Challenges and Moral Contemplations: Exploring the Obscure Skies
The Flight Way of Liability
As we graph the course into the eventual fate of flight, a variety of difficulties and moral contemplations arise not too far off. Resolving issues, for example, airspace blockage, protection worries in the time of independent flight, the natural effect of expanded air travel, and guaranteeing evenhanded admittance to arising advancements become basic. The moral elements of computer based intelligence in avionics, including responsibility, straightforwardness, and the likely dislodging of human jobs, request cautious thought.
This part explores the difficulties and moral contemplations that go with the fate of flight. As airspace turns out to be more blocked with UAM and independent vehicles, the requirement for powerful air traffic the board frameworks and administrative structures becomes principal. Security concerns related with the utilization of cutting edge observation advancements and the potential for information abuse in independent flight situations highlight the significance of moral contemplations in flying. The obligation to guarantee that the advantages of future flight innovations are circulated impartially and that natural maintainability stays a need directs the flight way into unfamiliar skies.

7.1   Technological innovations in the field of aviation and biomimicry

The field of avionics, portrayed by its persistent quest for development and headway, has tracked down motivation in the complicated movement of the normal world. Biomimicry, the imitating of organic frameworks and cycles in plan, has turned into a core value as aviation continued looking for effectiveness, maintainability, and execution. This investigation digs into the cooperative dance between mechanical developments in aeronautics and the artful dance of biomimicry, uncovering the manners by which nature's plans have impacted and upgraded the capacities of human flight.

1. Bird-Roused Flight: The Polish of Winged Authority
Taking Wing: From Quills to Ailerons
Birds, the undisputed bosses of the skies, have long intrigued flight pioneers. The plan standards of avian flight, from the construction of plumes to the mechanics of wing morphology, have motivated airplane architects to make more productive and flexibility flying machines.
This segment investigates what bird-propelled flight has meant for aeronautics innovation. The investigation of avian wing shapes, padded surfaces, and the complicated examples of wing stacking has educated the plan regarding airplane wings. For instance, the idea of winglets, enlivened by the tips of bird wings, has been integrated into current airplane to decrease drag and further develop eco-friendliness.

The variation of ailerons and folds, imitating the adjusted control surfaces of bird wings, improves the mobility and strength of planes. The journey for biomimetic flight reaches out past impersonation, meaning to open the insider facts of avian dominance to drive flying into a fate of improved execution and proficiency.

2. Bug Motivated Miniature Air Vehicles: Nature's Small Pilots
Microcosmic Flight: From Insects to MAVs

Bugs, with their unpredictable and proficient flight systems, have enlivened the improvement of Miniature Air Vehicles (MAVs) — little flying machines that duplicate the spryness and adaptability of their bug partners. From dragonflies to bugs, nature's little pilots grandstand surprising transformations that have turned into an outline for planning limited scope mechanical flyers.

This segment digs into the universe of bug roused MAVs. Specialists and analysts draw motivation from the interesting flight capacities of bugs, like dragonflies' dexterity and insects' versatility. The improvement of fluttering wing robots, displayed after bug flight, considers upgraded mobility and the capacity to explore complex conditions. The biomimetic way to deal with miniature air vehicles opens up opportunities for applications in observation, natural checking, and search-and-salvage missions, exhibiting how the complexities of bug flight can illuminate and change the universe of mechanical technology.

3. Shark Skin and Streamlined features: Smoothing out Trip with Nature's Plan
Smooth and Quick: From Sea Profundities to Streamlined Levels

Sharks, with their smoothed out bodies and one of a kind skin surface, have roused developments in streamlined features. The infinitesimal design of shark skin, portrayed by minuscule riblets that diminish drag, has been outfit to improve the proficiency of airplane and submerged vehicles.

This segment investigates the biomimetic uses of shark skin in flight. Engineers concentrating on the hydrodynamic effectiveness of shark scales have applied these standards to make riblet-covered surfaces on airplane wings. This biomimetic approach diminishes drag and further develops eco-friendliness by limiting the violent wind stream over the airplane. The interpretation of shark-propelled plan into avionics innovation epitomizes the exchange among biomimicry and streamlined features, where nature's smooth and quick plans guide the advancement of airplane surfaces.

4. The Owl's Quiet Flight: Sound Decrease in Avionics
Murmurs in the Evening: From Plumes to Calm Skies

Owls, famous for their quiet and covert flight, have turned into a wellspring of motivation for lessening clamor in flying.

The interesting construction of owl feathers and the transformation of their wing morphology add to a strikingly peaceful flight, giving bits of knowledge to moderating the commotion created via airplane.

This segment digs into what the owl's quiet flight has meant for sound decrease advances in aeronautics. The serrated driving edges of owl feathers disturb the tempestuous wind current that normally makes clamor. Analysts and specialists have investigated the fuse of serrations on airplane wing edges to diminish clamor during departure and landing. Biomimicry in sound decrease upgrades the traveler experience as well as addresses ecological worries connected with commotion contamination around air terminals, displaying how the subtleties of avian flight can rouse developments in making calmer skies.

5. Proficient Impetus: The Hummingbird's Fiery Tastefulness
Botanical Nectar to Stream Fuel: The Hummingbird's Flight Privileged insights

The hummingbird, with its capacity to float and move with extraordinary dexterity, has enlivened progressions in drive frameworks. Emulating the vivacious polish of hummingbird flight, analysts are investigating biomimetic ways to deal with make more proficient and flexibility robots and airplane.

This part investigates the biomimetic uses of hummingbird trip in drive frameworks. The extraordinary floating abilities of hummingbirds, accomplished through quick wing beats and exact control of wing movement, rouse the improvement of deft robots. The joining of fluttering wing instruments and bio-roused impetus frameworks intends to upgrade the productivity of automated aeronautical vehicles, empowering them to explore restricted spaces and perform assignments with unmatched accuracy. The hummingbird's flight mysteries offer a brief look into the capability of biomimicry in forming the fate of impetus innovation.

6. Organically Enlivened Independence: The Insight of Groups and Multitudes
Astuteness of the System: From Birds to Independent Frameworks

Noticing the aggregate knowledge of groups and multitudes in the regular world has affected the advancement of naturally roused independence in flight. The planned developments of birds and bugs give a model to planning independent frameworks equipped for cooperative direction and versatile reactions.

This segment dives into how the insight of herds and multitudes directs the advancement of independent frameworks. Biomimetic calculations, propelled by the decentralized dynamic cycles saw in nature, empower drones and independent vehicles to explore progressively evolving conditions. The use of multitude insight standards, got from the ways of behaving of social bugs, upgrades the proficiency and flexibility of independent frameworks.

The biomimetic reconciliation of aggregate knowledge offers a change in perspective in independent flying, opening the potential for cooperative and versatile ethereal frameworks.

7. Future Possibilities: An Embroidery Woven Naturally and Development Spreading out Wings of Tomorrow: Towards a Biomimetic Sky

As mechanical developments in flying keep on fitting with the expressive dance of biomimicry, the eventual fate of flight unfurls as an embroidery woven essentially and development. From bird-roused wings to bug enlivened advanced mechanics, from shark-motivated streamlined features to owl-propelled sound decrease, the marriage of science and innovation is reshaping the skies in manners that were once just longed for. This segment investigates the progressing and future possibilities of biomimicry in flying. As scientists dig further into the complexities of nature's plans, the potential for forward leaps in productivity, supportability, and execution becomes boundless. The combination of biomimetic standards with cutting edge materials, man-made reasoning, and feasible practices characterizes the direction of flying advancement. From metropolitan air versatility to space investigation, biomimicry turns into a core value in the spreading out wings of tomorrow, changing the manner in which we take off through the skies.

7.2   Human efforts to mimic nature's flight adaptations

The charm of flight, profoundly implanted in the human creative mind, has driven us to seek nature for motivation. From the smooth taking off of birds to the complex moves of bugs, the regular world has filled in as a material of development for those trying to imitate the class and productivity of airborne animals. This investigation dives into the entrancing domain of human endeavors to mirror nature's flight variations, uncovering the creativity, difficulties, and wins in our journey to take off with the very elegance as the animals that explore the skies.

1. Early Motivations: Icarus Dreams and Ornithopters
From Legend to Mechanics: Early Dreams of Flight

The craving to mirror nature's flight is just about as old as human progress itself. Legendary stories, like the account of Icarus, mirror mankind's longstanding interest with the fantasy of flight. Early creators and visionaries, roused by the easy trip of birds, looked to repeat nature's mechanics through gadgets known as ornithopters — machines intended to mirror the fluttering movement of bird wings.

This segment investigates the early motivations that powered human endeavors to emulate nature's flight. From old legends that discussed wings made from plumes and wax to the plans of Leonardo da Vinci, who portrayed ornithopter ideas in the fifteenth hundred years, the fantasy of human flight came to fruition.

While these early undertakings confronted impediments in materials and impetus, they laid the foundation for future trend-setters to draw motivation from the mechanics of avian headway.

2. Fixed-Wing Airplane: Divulging the Privileged insights of Taking off
Wright Siblings and Then some: Bridling Lift and Push

The leap forward into maintained and controlled flight accompanied the appearance of fixed-wing airplane. The Wright siblings, Orville and Wilbur, accomplished this achievement in 1903 with their famous trip at Kitty Falcon, North Carolina. Propelled by the life systems of birds and their comprehension of lift and pushed, the Wright siblings planned and constructed the main effective controlled plane, everlastingly redirecting human transportation.

This segment digs into how the standards of nature's flight transformations, especially the authority of lift and pushed, impacted the advancement of fixed-wing airplane. The aerofoil state of bird wings filled in as a plan for wing plan, while the propeller emulated the rotational movement of avian wings. The Wright siblings' prosperity denoted the start of another time in flying, with human flight turning into a reality and making way for additional progressions.

3. Helicopters: Vertical Rising and Drifting Motivation
Rotors and Whirligigs: Getting from Drifting Dominance

While fixed-wing airplane overwhelmed the skies, the mission to copy nature's flight stretched out to vertical climb and floating — a domain where helicopters arose as the mechanical encapsulation of nature's drifting dominance, as found in hummingbirds and other light-footed fliers.

This segment investigates how helicopters, with their pivoting edges and vertical departure abilities, were propelled commonly's floating animals. The special flight capacities of hummingbirds, which can float in mid-air with staggering accuracy, filled in as a model for engineers looking to accomplish comparative accomplishments in airplane. The plan of helicopter rotors and the capacity to drift, rise, and slip upward were impressions of nature's elevated trapeze artists, displaying how human inventiveness kept on drawing from the biomechanics of flying living beings.

4. VTOL and VTOL-roused Innovations: Ascending Higher than ever
In an upward direction Taking Off: Imitating Avian Nimbleness

Vertical Departure and Landing (VTOL) advances, motivated commonly's agile fliers, have become essential in avionics, especially in the improvement of military airplane, drones, and metropolitan air versatility arrangements. Getting from the deftness of birds and bugs, human designers look to duplicate the capacity to climb and slide upward, opening additional opportunities for mobility.

This segment dives into how VTOL advances draw motivation from nature's flight variations. Flying predators, equipped for fast departures and exact arrivals, impact the plan of military planes and robots. Metropolitan air versatility ideas, imagining air taxicabs and individual air vehicles, are roused by the mastery of birds exploring thick metropolitan conditions. VTOL advancements, whether as tiltrotors, vectored push, or imaginative rotor plans, feature the continuous endeavors to imitate the adaptability of nature's pilots.

5. Biomimetic Wing Plans: Past Plumes and Ailerons
Adaptability and Versatility: Transforming Wings and Then some

The journey to imitate nature's flight has prompted progressions in biomimetic wing plans. Enlivened by the adaptability and versatility of bird wings, scientists and specialists investigate the potential outcomes of transforming wings that can powerfully change shape during flight, further developing productivity and mobility.

This part investigates the biomimetic developments in wing plan. The adaptability of bird wings, which can change shape because of various flight conditions, fills in as a model for creating versatile wing advances. Imitating the manner in which birds change the situating of their quills in flight, these biomimetic wings can possibly improve airplane execution, lessen drag, and enhance proficiency. The development from fixed-wing plans to dynamic, shape-changing wings mirrors the continuous work to open the privileged insights of nature's flight.

6. Bio-Motivated Drive: Outfitting Nature's Propulsive Effectiveness
From Birdsong to Sonic Blasts: Impetus Mimicry

Impetus frameworks in flight have additionally been impacted ordinarily's productive strategies for creating push. From the quiet and strong fluttering of bird wings to the supersonic paces accomplished by specific species, people have tried to saddle nature's propulsive proficiency for more reasonable and superior execution airplane.

This part investigates how bio-propelled impetus has formed flight. The quiet trip of owls, accomplished through particular wing and quill structures, has enlivened the plan of calmer airplane motors. Sonic blasts, made by specific birds during plunges, act as a kind of perspective for engineers looking to comprehend and moderate the sonic impacts of supersonic flight. The investigation of nature's drive instruments gives significant experiences to streamlining airplane motors, diminishing ecological effect, and accomplishing higher rates.

7. Independence and simulated intelligence: Nature's Route Astuteness
Mental Sky: Exploring with Avian Sense

Nature's guides, from transitory birds to bugs, have motivated the advancement of independent frameworks and man-made consciousness (man-made intelligence) in flying. Drawing from the natural and versatile ways of behaving saw in the collective of animals, human specialists plan to make smart airplane that can explore complex conditions, pursue continuous choices, and adjust to evolving conditions.

This segment investigates how independence and computer based intelligence in avionics are enlivened naturally's route astuteness. Transient birds, fit for undertaking significant distance ventures with accuracy, impact the improvement of independent route frameworks. The aggregate knowledge saw in groups of birds and multitudes of bugs turns into a model for planning artificial intelligence calculations that empower cooperative dynamic in independent robots. As human undertakings move towards making mental skies, the illustrations from nature's pilots guide the improvement of canny and versatile flight frameworks.

7.3   Ethical considerations and environmental impact of emerging flight technologies

The investigation of arising flight advances divulges a heavenward skyline loaded up with commitment, development, and groundbreaking prospects. In any case, as we leave on this excursion of flying progression, it is critical to examine the moral contemplations and ecological effect that go with the advancement of flight. This investigation dives into the moral obligations borne by the makers and clients of arising flight innovations, tending to the ethical quandaries and natural results that request cautious route.

1. Moral Contemplations in Aeronautics: Adjusting Progress and Obligation
The Ethical Horizon: Moral Problems in Flight

As innovation impels flying into new domains, moral contemplations come to the bleeding edge, molding the dependable turn of events and organization of arising flight advances. From the utilization of man-made reasoning to worries about protection, security, and the cultural ramifications of cutting edge airborne capacities, the moral scene of aeronautics requests conscious consideration.

This segment analyzes the moral contemplations that emerge in the domain of avionics. The coordination of man-made reasoning into flight frameworks brings up issues about responsibility, straightforwardness, and the potential for predisposition in direction. Protection concerns arise as reconnaissance innovations advance, testing the sensitive harmony among security and individual opportunities. Guaranteeing the wellbeing of travelers, spectators, and administrators becomes principal as independent and automated frameworks take to the skies.

The moral horizon of flight requires steady investigation, with partners exploring the perplexing convergence of mechanical advancement and moral obligation.

2. Security in the Period of Flying Observation: Finding Some kind of harmony
Eyes overhead: Airborne Reconnaissance and Protection

The ascent of automated ethereal vehicles (UAVs) and reconnaissance innovations presents a blade that cuts both ways with regards to protection. While these progressions offer phenomenal capacities for checking and information assortment, they additionally raise worries about observation overextend, attack of individual space, and the potential for abuse.

This part digs into the moral contemplations encompassing aeronautical reconnaissance and protection. The utilization of robots for reconnaissance, whether by policing, organizations, or confidential elements, prompts conversations about the limits of individual security. Finding some kind of harmony between the advantages of reconnaissance for public wellbeing and the security of individual privileges turns into a basic moral test. Guidelines, straightforwardness, and public talk are fundamental parts of exploring the moral components of elevated reconnaissance in a way that regards individual security.

3. Independent Frameworks and Responsibility: The Job of Human Oversight
Past Pilots: Exploring Independence and Obligation

The rise of independent flight frameworks presents another outskirts of moral contemplations, especially in regards to responsibility and the job of human oversight. As machines take on progressively complex dynamic cycles, questions emerge about who bears liability in case of blunders, mishaps, or moral situations.

This segment investigates the moral difficulties related with independent flight. While independence guarantees improved productivity and wellbeing, the absence of a human pilot brings up issues about responsibility and the capacity to settle on morally informed choices. Laying out systems for human oversight, characterizing the constraints of independent direction, and deciding risk in case of episodes become urgent moral contemplations. Finding some kind of harmony between the advantages of independence and the requirement for dependable dynamic remaining parts a focal topic in the moral scene of arising flight advances.

4. Ecological Effect of Flying: Exploring the Carbon Skyprint
Eco-Accommodating Skies: Tending to the Carbon Impression

The natural effect of flight, especially regarding fossil fuel byproducts and environmental results, remains as a huge moral concern.

The development of air travel, combined with the extension of metropolitan air portability and space the travel industry, requires a basic assessment of the business' carbon impression and its commitment to environmental change.

This segment dives into the natural morals of avionics, underscoring the carbon skyprint and its suggestions for the planet. Conventional aeronautics, controlled by petroleum products, contributes significantly to ozone harming substance emanations. The approach of electric and cross breed electric airplane, alongside economical avionics fills, offers likely answers for moderate the ecological effect. Moral contemplations rotate around the business' liability to embrace eco-accommodating advances, put resources into manageable practices, and add to worldwide endeavors to battle environmental change. Adjusting the accommodation of air head out with the basic to safeguard the climate turns into a moral basic in the continuous development of flight advances.

5. Manageable Flying Fills: Impelling Moral Decisions for What's in store
Green Impetus: Moral Contemplations in Fuel Decisions

The quest for supportable flying powers (SAFs) arises as a critical moral thought in tending to the natural effect of flight. As the business looks for options in contrast to customary non-renewable energy sources, the determination and execution of eco-accommodating drive advances become fundamental to moral direction.

This segment investigates the moral components of taking on manageable flying fills. SAFs, got from inexhaustible sources like plant biomass, squander materials, or manufactured processes fueled by sustainable power, offer a pathway to diminish the carbon impression of flight. Moral contemplations incorporate the harmony between food creation and biofuel crops, the general life cycle outflows of elective fills, and the fair conveyance of the natural weight. The capable joining of manageable flight powers into the flying business mirrors a promise to moral dynamic in the mission for greener skies.

6. Metropolitan Air Portability: Exploring the Moral Horizon of City Flight
Over the City: Metropolitan Air Portability and Moral Urbanism

The idea of Metropolitan Air Portability (UAM), imagining air cabs and individual ethereal vehicles, presents an exceptional arrangement of moral contemplations with regards to metropolitan scenes. As the skies above urban communities become possible center points for aeronautical transportation, questions emerge about commotion contamination, wellbeing, openness, and the evenhanded circulation of these arising innovations.

This segment looks at the moral ramifications of UAM in metropolitan conditions. The combination of air taxicabs and individual air vehicles raises worries about clamor levels, as well as the effect of expanded air traffic on the personal satisfaction for occupants.

Guaranteeing wellbeing norms, creating strong air traffic the board frameworks, and resolving issues of availability and reasonableness become moral objectives. Exploring the metropolitan horizon morally includes a cooperative exertion among policymakers, innovation designers, and the networks impacted by the presentation of metropolitan air portability.

7. Space The travel industry: Moral Outskirts Past Earth's Air
Past the Blue: Morals in the Time of Room The travel industry

The expanding field of room the travel industry presents moral contemplations that stretch out past the limits of Earth's environment. As privately owned businesses and people adventure into space, questions emerge about security, ecological effect, and the capable utilization of extraterrestrial assets.

This part investigates the moral boondocks of room the travel industry. Guaranteeing the security of room vacationers, both on the way and during spaceflights, turns into an essential moral concern. The natural effect of rocket dispatches and space travel brings up issues about manageability and the drawn out results of human exercises in space. Moreover, moral contemplations reach out to the mindful utilization of divine bodies and the protection of space as a common asset. As space the travel industry advances, moral structures should be laid out to direct capable practices past Earth's environment.

Chapter 8
Conclusion

In the sweeping excursion through the pages of "Elevated Expressive dance: The Craftsmanship and Study of Flight Transformations," we have set out on a dazzling investigation of the different, entrancing universe of flight. From the rich movement of birds in avian greatness to the multifaceted expressive dance of bug flying, and from the taking off magnificence of bats at the center of attention to the ethereal dreams of human flight, our journey has unfurled like an ensemble in the skies, mixing the workmanship and study of elevated transformations.

Thinking about the Embroidery of Flight

As we think about the embroidery woven with the strings of avian authority, bug resourcefulness, and human goal, the general subject that arises is the consistent combination of workmanship and science in the domain of flight transformations. The skies, when a distant material, have turned into a phase for a marvelous artful dance where organic entities of different beginnings exhibit their flying ability. Every part of this investigation has divulged the unpredictable systems, transformative wonders, and mechanical developments that add to the ensemble of flight.

The Exchange of Workmanship and Science

At the core of "Elevated Expressive dance" lies the exchange among craftsmanship and science. The class of a bird in flight, the many-sided dance of bugs on the breeze, the quiet nighttime artful dance of bats, and the mechanical wonders driving human flight — all are articulations of both the imaginative magnificence and the logical accuracy intrinsic in the realm of flying. The fastidious variations made by development and the cunning developments brought about by human personalities unite to make an agreeable artful dance in the skies.

Disclosing the Moral and Ecological Aspects

Notwithstanding, our investigation goes past the sheer miracle of flight; it digs into the moral contemplations and natural effect woven into the texture of arising flight advances. The skies, once apparently boundless, presently convey the heaviness of obligation as humankind arrives at new levels. The moral situations encompassing independence, protection, and responsibility, as well as the environmental impression of flying, help us that the pursuit to remember flight accompanies a significant obligation to explore the skies with principles and care.

The Obligation of Advancement

In the finishing up demonstration of our excursion, we stand at the crossing point of advancement and obligation. The progressions in flight advances, from biomimicry to independent frameworks, request that we explore the skies morally. The moral contemplations featured in our investigation highlight the requirement for honest direction, guideline, and a pledge to cultural prosperity as we unfurl the wings of tomorrow.

Adjusting Progress and Conservation

The moral contemplations in flying reverberation a key truth: progress in flight should be offset with the conservation of moral standards. As we embrace independence, observation innovations, and metropolitan air portability, it is basic to protect individual security, guarantee responsibility, and address the cultural ramifications of these groundbreaking advancements. The skies, once free and unknown, presently require moral route graphs that guide us through the neglected regions of capable advancement.

Gatekeepers of the Skies: Maintainability and Obligation

The ecological effect of aeronautics, featured in our investigation, accentuates the requirement for maintainable practices in the mission for flight. The carbon skyprint, an unmistakable indication of the environmental results of customary flight, requires a shift toward supportable flying fills, electric drive, and eco-accommodating innovations. The obligation to be gatekeepers of the skies stretches out to limiting the ecological impression of our ethereal undertakings and protecting the fragile equilibrium of our planet.

Human Flight: A Conversion of Dreams and Reality

Human flight, when the domain of legend and creative mind, has turned into a substantial reality. The set of experiences and development of human flight, investigated exhaustively, uncover the unstoppable soul of investigation and the tenacious quest for the skies. From the fantasies of Icarus to the mechanical wonders of current flight, the human mission to take off like birds has risen above creative mind and become a fundamental piece of our existence.

The Convergence of Workmanship and Science in Human Flight

The investigation of human flight not just dives into the mechanical headways and verifiable achievements yet in addition underlines the convergence of workmanship and science in this unprecedented accomplishment. The plan of airplane, the designing of drive frameworks, and the sheer delight of flight itself structure a material where human imagination combines with logical creativity.

As we explore the skies, the tradition of human flight turns into a demonstration of our capacity to connect the domains of creative mind and accomplishment.

The Artful dance of Relocation: Exploring the Unexplored world

The expressive dance of relocation, an entrancing dance across mainlands and through seasons, reveals the insider facts of significant distance flight. Our investigation of movement designs, route signals, and the difficulties looked by transient species highlights the interconnectedness of biological systems and the requirement for protection. The expressive dance of movement, a characteristic peculiarity idealized over centuries, fills in as an aide for moral contemplations even with ecological changes and human mediations.

Trip from now on: Spreading out Wings of Tomorrow

The last venture of our investigation slings us into the fate of flight — a domain where mechanical developments, moral contemplations, and ecological supportability merge. The spreading out wings of tomorrow coax us to embrace a dream of flight that blends with the climate, focuses on wellbeing, and maintains moral standards. The orchestra of trip from here on out, directed by development and obligation, turns into a demonstration of our aggregate creative mind, development, and the unstoppable soul to investigate the unexplored world.

The Continuous Orchestra of Advancement and Nature's Direction

In the continuous ensemble of development, human endeavors to impersonate nature's flight transformations stand as a demonstration of our capacity to learn, adjust, and take off to new skylines. Whether drawing motivation from the easy trip of birds or the unpredictable moves of bugs, our undertakings to duplicate nature's dominance mirror a significant affirmation of the insight encoded in the regular world. The artful dance of biomimicry turns into a choreographer, directing the developments of airplane, drones, and independent frameworks with the class consummated by a long period of time of development.

Exploring the Skies Mindfully: Moral Contemplations and Ecological Effect of Arising Flight Advances

The investigation of moral contemplations and ecological effect highlights the requirement for mindful advancement in the skies. As we explore the skies capably, we should blend progress with moral standards, address cultural worries, and relieve the environmental impression of flight. The continuous ensemble of flight requires a guarantee to straightforwardness, responsibility, and an all encompassing methodology that considers the cultural, natural, and moral elements of flying development.

8.1   Summarizing key concepts in aerial ballet

In the great embroidery of "Flying Expressive dance: The Workmanship and Study of Flight Variations," a heap of key ideas dance across the pages, each adding to the orchestra of grasping in the realm of flight. From the developmental miracles of avian greatness to the multifaceted moves of bug flying, and from the quiet nighttime artful dance of bats to the ethereal dreams of human flight, these ideas wind around together a story that embraces both the imaginativeness and the logical accuracy of flight transformations. As we disentangle the complexities, we should investigate and sum up the key ideas that characterize the captivating universe of airborne artful dance.

1. Avian Greatness: The Bosses of the Sky
Key Idea: Developmental Authority in Bird Flight

The avian domain remains as a demonstration of the dominance of flight variations sharpened more than large number of long periods of development. Birds, with their assorted wing shapes, feather structures, and concentrated respiratory frameworks, represent the apex of aeronautical greatness. The critical idea here lies in understanding the transformative cycles that have etched birds into the unmatched experts of the sky.

From the empty bones that ease up their edges to the unpredictably planned feathers that work with lift and mobility, avian flight variations are a wonder of regular designing. The idea stretches out to the variety of flight systems seen in different bird species, from the taking off greatness of hawks to the nimble exciting bends in the road of hummingbirds. Every variation is a finely tuned reaction to the particular biological specialties and endurance challenges that different bird species face.

2. Bug Air transportation: The Expressive dance of the Small scale Flyers
Key Idea: Dominance in Limited scope Flight

The universe of bugs presents an idea of trip on a smaller than expected scale, where accuracy and spryness become the overwhelming focus. The vital idea here lies in understanding the biomechanics and one of a kind variations that permit bugs to explore the air with unmatched artfulness. From the unpredictable wing developments of dragonflies to the drifting capacities of honey bees, bug aviation grandstands the imaginativeness and effectiveness of trip in the little domain.

The idea stretches out to the flexibility of flight methodologies utilized by bugs for endurance, including skimming, drifting, and fast shifts in course. The intricacies of bug flight, frequently directed by tactile variations and unpredictable wing structures, feature the versatility and productivity important for life in different biological systems. Bug air transportation fills in as a wellspring of motivation for human-designed advances, especially in the improvement of Miniature Air Vehicles (MAVs).

3. Bosses of the Sky: Bats At the center of attention
Key Idea: Nighttime Flight and Echolocation
Bats, frequently misjudged and undervalued, become the overwhelming focus as the
nighttime maestros of the ethereal expressive dance. The critical idea here lies in
understanding the special variations that empower bats to flourish in obscurity, using
echolocation as a route device. The dominance of trip in bats difficulties our
predispositions about nighttime animals and highlights the variety of transformative
answers for the difficulties of airborne life.
The idea stretches out to the life structures and physiology of bat flight, described by
prolonged fingers and an adaptable wing layer. Bats grandstand the adaptability of flight
transformations, changing flawlessly between dexterous moves and extremely long
travel. Their job as fundamental pollinators and bug regulators further underscores the
environmental significance of these nighttime airborne artists.

4. Human Flight: Connecting Creative mind and Reality
Key Idea: History, Advancement, and the Crossing point of Craftsmanship and
Science
The idea of human flight isn't simply a verifiable story however a living demonstration of
the union of creative mind and mechanical development. From the legendary dreams of
Icarus to the momentous accomplishments of the Wright siblings, the vital idea here lies
in the nonstop quest for trip as an image of human goal. Human flight delivers the
convergence of craftsmanship and science, where the plan of airplane turns into a
material for both inventiveness and designing accuracy.
The idea stretches out to the advancement of aeronautics, set apart by achievements,
for example, the principal controlled flight, the improvement of business air travel, and
the investigation of room. Human flight isn't just a mechanical accomplishment; it is an
indication of the human soul's unyielding craving to arrive at new levels and investigate
the skies. The continuous adventure of human flight keeps on motivating ages, advising
us that the skies are not restricts however solicitations to dream and investigate.

5. Biomimicry: Nature as A definitive Specialist
Key Idea: Acquiring from Nature's Plans
Biomimicry arises as a key idea that rises above individual species, enveloping the
more extensive thought of drawing motivation from nature's plans to tackle human
difficulties. The critical idea here lies in perceiving nature as a definitive designer, giving
a plan to creative arrangements in different fields, particularly in flight. From the
streamlined standards roused by bird wings to the independent route systems gathered
from transient examples, biomimicry is a core value in the flying expressive dance.

The idea stretches out to the improvement of advances that emulate nature's productivity, versatility, and polish. Biomimicry isn't just about recreating outer structures however understanding the fundamental rules that have advanced over ages. It fills in as an extension between the regular world and human creativity, offering arrangements that are compelling as well as manageable, repeating the standards of nature itself.

6. Moral Contemplations and Natural Effect
Key Idea: Capable Development in the Skies

The investigation of moral contemplations and ecological effect is a critical idea that underscores the obligation that accompanies propelling flight innovations. The vital idea here lies in grasping the fragile harmony among progress and protection. As independence, reconnaissance advancements, and metropolitan air versatility become basic pieces of the aeronautics scene, moral independent direction becomes basic.
The idea stretches out to the ecological effect of flight, especially the carbon impression and the mission for supportable practices. Moral contemplations feature the requirement for straightforwardness, responsibility, and an all encompassing methodology that considers the cultural, ecological, and moral elements of flying development. Capable development in the skies turns into a core value, guaranteeing that the expressive dance of flight unfurls with care and thought for the world we possess.

7. The Artful dance of Movement: Exploring the Unexplored world
Key Idea: Examples, Route, and Preservation

The idea of the artful dance of movement incorporates the striking excursions of flying species across huge distances. The vital idea here lies in understanding the examples, route signals, and the difficulties looked by transitory species as they cross mainlands and explore the unexplored world. Relocation fills in as a demonstration of the interconnectedness of environments and the requirement for protection endeavors to defend these unprecedented ethereal excursions.
The idea stretches out to the job of route and ecological prompts in significant distance flight, underlining the dependence of transient species on heavenly milestones, attractive fields, and geographical elements. Preservation difficulties and arrangements become basic to the idea, encouraging mankind to assume a part in safeguarding the territories and conditions that empower these exceptional relocations.

8.2 Reflection on the interconnectedness of art and science in the study of flight adaptations

The investigation of flight transformations isn't just a logical undertaking; it is a sensitive dance where workmanship and science spin as one, making a hypnotizing movement that unfurls in the skies.

The interconnectedness of workmanship and science in the investigation of flight transformations uncovers a significant beneficial interaction, where the polish of nature's plans meets the accuracy of logical request. In this reflection, we dig into the complicated strides of this dance, investigating how craftsmanship and science combine to make a rich embroidery of grasping in the ethereal artful dance.

1. The Tasteful Orchestra of Avian Greatness:

In the domain of avian flight, craftsmanship and science fit consistently. The tasteful excellence of a bird in flight, with its wings outstretched against the material of the sky, rises above the limits of logical examination. The multifaceted examples of quills, the smooth curves of wings, and the easy moves of airborne trapeze artistry are articulations of a creative work of art molded by a long period of time of development. However, underneath this tasteful orchestra lies the fastidious accuracy of logical standards. The aerofoil state of bird wings, the empty bones that diminish weight, and the complexities of quill structures all observe the laws of material science and biomechanics. Science uncovers the mysteries of lift, push, and optimal design that coordinate the avian artful dance. The interconnectedness of craftsmanship and science in avian flight grandstands the polish of nature's plan and the fundamental logical rules that administer this airborne expressive dance.

2. Bug Aviation: Minute Wonders in Flight:

The artful dance of bug flight acquaints us with a small scale existence where creativity and logical resourcefulness dance connected at the hip. The sensitive vacillate of a butterfly, the accuracy of a bumble bee's dance, and the entrancing flight examples of dragonflies are demonstration of the creativity imbued in the bug domain.
According to a creative point of view, the lively varieties and perplexing wing examples of bugs add a layer of visual verse to their flight. The sheer variety of shapes and sizes among bug wings exhibits nature's imagination at its best. However, as we dig into the logical domain, we uncover the complexities of bug flight components. The moment changes of wing beats, the fast shifts in course, and the utilization of tactile transformations for route all mirror the accuracy of logical variations sharpened by advancement. The interconnectedness of workmanship and science in bug air transportation paints a material where excellence and usefulness blend in a hypnotizing show.

3. Bats: Nighttime Choreographers In obscurity:

Bats, the nighttime choreographers of the skies, exemplify a dance where creativity and logical transformation converge in the shroud of dimness. The quiet trip of bats, joined by the ethereal reverberations of echolocation, adds a layer of persona to their flying expressive dance.

According to a creative point of view, seeing bats outlined against the twilight sky or executing gymnastic moves in quest for prey is completely a nighttime expressive dance.

The logical complexities of bat flight uncover a developmental dance finely tuned for the difficulties of the evening. The prolonged fingers and adaptable wing films, frequently clouded by the obscurity, add to the imaginativeness of their flight. All the while, the refined utilization of echolocation, a logical wonder, highlights the accuracy expected for route and hunting without any light. Bats represent how the interconnectedness of workmanship and science in flight transformations stretches out even to the secrets of the evening.

4. Human Flight: Crossing over Dreams and Mechanical Real factors:

Human flight, a demonstration of both creative mind and designing ability, is a domain where workmanship and science meet to transform dreams into the real world. The notable picture of a bird in flight has propelled craftsmen and visionaries for quite a long time, and as people took to the skies, the fantasy turned into a material for mechanical development.

From an imaginative stance, seeing an airplane taking off through the mists is a visual ensemble that repeats the smooth bends of avian flight. The plan of airplane, the play of light on wings, and the sheer wonderment of opposing gravity all add to the imaginative story of human flight. At the same time, the study of optimal design, impetus frameworks, and designing accuracy impels these airborne marvels into the domains of the real world. The interconnectedness of workmanship and science in human flight is a demonstration of the unyielding human soul that tries to copy the verse of nature's pilots.

5. Biomimicry: Nature as the Dream for Advancement:

Biomimicry remains as a scaffold between the tastefulness of nature's plans and the down to earth universe of human development. The idea spins around drawing motivation from nature's answers for tackle human difficulties. From the plan of airplane wings to the improvement of independent frameworks, biomimicry embodies the interconnected dance of craftsmanship and science.

The creative appeal of biomimicry lies in the imitating of nature's structures. Specialists and planners frequently track down motivation in the smooth shapes of birds, the productive drive of bugs, or the versatile methodologies of bats. At the same time, the logical center of biomimicry dives into understanding the fundamental rules that make these variations effective. The dance of workmanship and science in biomimicry turns into a cooperative exertion, where nature fills in as the dream for human development.

6. Moral Contemplations: Adjusting Progress and Obligation:

In the developing scene of flight advances, moral contemplations arise as a directing power that explores the sensitive harmony among progress and obligation. The interconnected dance of craftsmanship and science reaches out to the moral domain, where the cultural effect of arising innovations turns into a material for moral consideration.

According to an imaginative viewpoint, moral contemplations welcome us to imagine a future where the skies are mechanically cutting-edge as well as morally sound. The artistic creation of this future includes contemplations of protection, wellbeing, and the cultural ramifications of independent frameworks. At the same time, the study of morals dives into the nuanced conversations of responsibility, straightforwardness, and the ethical obligations related with the development of flight advancements. The dance of workmanship and science in moral contemplations makes a structure that guarantees the expressive dance of flight unfurls with care and cultural prosperity.

7. The Expressive dance of Movement: Nature's Airborne Ensemble:

The idea of movement epitomizes a stupendous expressive dance coordinated essentially itself. Birds navigating landmasses, bugs setting out on incredible excursions, and the interconnected biological systems that help these relocations make a striking exhibition. The dance of workmanship and science in relocation mirrors the interconnectedness of species, the dependence on ecological prompts, and the basic of preservation.

According to an imaginative viewpoint, the expressive dance of movement is a living embroidery that paints the skies with the dynamic shades of different species moving. The sheer scale and synchronicity of these relocations add a layer of regular magnificence to the dance. At the same time, the study of movement disentangles the secrets of heavenly route, the dependence on Earth's attractive fields, and the interconnected trap of biological systems that support these excursions. The dance of workmanship and science in movement is a demonstration of the complicated movement of nature's elevated orchestra.

Reflection: The Dance Go on in the Skies:

As we consider the interconnectedness of craftsmanship and science in the investigation of flight variations, it becomes clear that this dance is progressing — a ceaseless artful dance that unfurls in the skies. Nature, as a definitive choreographer, keeps on moving specialists, researchers, and trend-setters the same. The dance of craftsmanship and science isn't bound to the pages of a book or the walls of a research center; it stretches out to the huge scope of the skies, where every animal, every airplane, and every development turns into an artist in this everlasting expressive dance.

The interconnectedness of workmanship and science in flight transformations welcomes us to see the value in the excellence of the skies while diving into the logical complexities that make flight conceivable. A dance rises above disciplines, where the craftsman and the researcher figure out some shared interest chasing understanding and appreciation for the miracles of flight. As the dance proceeds, let us embrace the cooperative energy of craftsmanship and science, permitting it to push us into new domains of disclosure and appreciation for the expressive dance that unfurls above us.

8.3   The ongoing quest to unravel the mysteries of aerial ballet and its impact on the natural world

The unlimited field of the sky fills in as a material for a never-ending expressive dance — a dynamic and complicated presentation arranged by the occupants of the air. As we dive into the continuous mission to disentangle the secrets of elevated expressive dance, we end up on an odyssey that rises above the domains of science, craftsmanship, and biological interconnectedness. This investigation isn't simply a scholastic pursuit; an excursion tries to figure out the significant effect of flight variations on the normal world, disentangling the mysteries of the airborne domain and its biological importance.

1. The Dance of Development: Disclosing the Starting points of Flying Expressive dance

The secrets of elevated expressive dance track down their foundations in the fabulous embroidery of development — a story prearranged over ages. The continuous journey to comprehend flight variations digs into the transformative dance that has molded the assorted systems seen in birds, bugs, bats, and even people.

Avian Class: An Orchestra of Transformative Dominance

The development of avian flight remains as a demonstration of the persevering drive for variation and endurance. The continuous journey to disentangle the secrets of avian artful dance includes following the developmental strides that changed padded dinosaurs into the padded wonders that effortlessness our skies today. Understanding the particular tensions that inclined toward productive flight and the mind boggling variations that arose over the long run gives a brief look into the continuous developmental expressive dance that shapes avian greatness.

Bug Air transportation: Small Wonders in Transformative Flight

Bugs, with their different shapes and sizes, participate in an artful dance of flight transformations that has developed north of millions of years. The continuous mission to disentangle the secrets of bug flight brings us into the multifaceted universe of exoskeletons, wing structures, and tangible variations.

From dragonflies executing ethereal trapeze artistry to honey bees performing exact moves in the air, the continuous investigation of bug flight reveals the developmental artful dance of scaled down wonders that add to natural equilibrium and biodiversity.

Bats: Nighttime Expressive dance in the Shadows of Advancement
Bats, the nighttime choreographers of the skies, carry an interesting aspect to the continuous mission for figuring out flight variations. Their development is a story of adjusting to the difficulties of evening time presence and dominating the utilization of echolocation — a type of natural sonar. The continuous investigation of bat flight includes unwinding the hereditary dance that led to their unmistakable wing structures and the brain ensemble that coordinates their nighttime route.

Human Flight: An Innovative Expressive dance Roused Ordinarily
The continuous mission to disentangle the secrets of flying expressive dance reaches out to the domain of human flight — a story not written in qualities but rather created through development. From the legendary dreams of Icarus to the innovative wonders of current avionics, understanding the development of human flight includes following the strides of innovators, architects, and pilots. The continuous investigation discloses the mechanical artful dance where nature's standards are imitated and, at times, outperformed to vanquish the skies.

2. Biological Effect: The Far reaching influence of Ethereal Expressive dance in Nature
Past the logical complexities of flight variations lies the natural effect of ethereal expressive dance — a peculiarity that reaches out a long ways past the singular entertainers. The continuous journey to disentangle the secrets of flight includes translating the environmental meaning of airborne animals and their commitment to the fragile equilibrium of biological systems.

Avian Environment Specialists: The Wings that Shape Living spaces
Birds, with their different flight variations, assume a vital part in molding biological systems. The continuous investigation of avian artful dance includes understanding how birds go about as environment engineers, affecting vegetation designs, seed dispersal, and bug populaces. From the superb raptors that keep up with hunter prey equilibrium to the pollinators that work with the generation of blossoming plants, the environmental effect of avian flight swells through earthly scenes.

Bug Flight: Fertilization, Nuisance Control, and Biodiversity
Bugs, frequently disregarded in their flying undertakings, contribute fundamentally to biological system administrations through their flight variations.

The continuous mission to unwind the secrets of bug flight includes perceiving their job as pollinators, fundamental for the propagation of many blossoming plants. Moreover, the artful dance of bug flight incorporates the normal nuisance control administrations given by ruthless bugs, adding to the guideline of bug populaces and the upkeep of biodiversity.

Bats as Natural Stewards of the Evening
Bats, frequently connected with the puzzling and the nighttime, arise as biological stewards of the evening. The continuous investigation of bat flight includes unraveling their effect on bug populaces, especially those that present agrarian dangers. By controlling bug bothers, bats add to farming maintainability and decrease the requirement for synthetic mediations. The biological artful dance of bats reaches out to their job as pollinators, further underscoring their significance in keeping up with the strength of environments.

Human Flight and its Biological Impression
Human flight, pushed by motors and driven by mechanical development, has a particular natural effect. The continuous mission to comprehend the biological outcomes of human flight includes surveying the carbon impression, commotion contamination, and living space disturbance related with aeronautics. From the rambling organizations of air terminals to the contrails left overhead, human flight leaves an engraving on the climate. The continuous investigation digs into alleviating this effect through headways in manageable avionics energizes, electric drive, and eco-accommodating advancements.

3. Biomimicry: Developments Propelled Essentially's Elevated Expressive dance
The continuous journey to unwind the secrets of airborne expressive dance reaches out past comprehension and valuing the normal entertainers; it motivates development. Biomimicry, the act of drawing motivation from nature's plans, fills in as a scaffold between the continuous investigation of flight variations and the improvement of state of the art advancements.

Bird-Roused Flight: Airplane as Padded Trailblazers
The continuous journey for biomimicry in aeronautics includes concentrating on the flight transformations of birds to upgrade the effectiveness and manageability of airplane. From the streamlined forms of wings to the unique changes made during flight, airplane configuration is progressively affected by the continuous investigation of avian expressive dance. The copying of bird-propelled flight works on the presentation of airplane as well as lessens fuel utilization and natural effect.

Bug Roused Miniature Air Vehicles: Nature's Accuracy in Innovation
Bug flight, with its accuracy and nimbleness, fills in as a diagram for the continuous improvement of Miniature Air Vehicles (MAVs). The continuous mission for biomimicry in innovation includes concentrating on the flight variations of bugs to make deft and flexibility drones. The mimicry of bug roused flight empowers the continuous advancement of aeronautical vehicles that can explore complex conditions, watch scenes, and add to different logical and modern applications.

Bats as Models for Independent Frameworks: Echolocation in Innovation
Bats, with their authority of echolocation, motivate continuous investigation into independent route frameworks. The continuous mission for biomimicry in innovation includes concentrating on the brain components behind bat echolocation to foster modern independent frameworks. The imitating of bat-motivated route not just upgrades the abilities of automated flying vehicles (UAVs) yet additionally finds applications in fields like mechanical technology and reconnaissance.

4. The Dance Proceeds: Elevated Expressive dance from now on
As we explore the continuous mission to disentangle the secrets of airborne expressive dance, our look moves in the direction representing things to come — a consistently extending skyline where science, development, and natural stewardship merge. The continuous investigation of flight variations fills in as a compass directing us toward a future where the artful dance in the skies keeps on enthralling, rouse, and add to the prosperity of the planet.

Innovative Headways: Preparing for Maintainable Flight
The continuous mission for reasonable aeronautics includes mechanical progressions that address the ecological effect of flight. From electric drive frameworks to the improvement of biofuels, the continuous investigation of flight variations motivates developments that prepare for a more supportable future in flying. The dance of innovation and nature unfurls as specialists and designers endeavor to adjust the appeal of trip with the basic of ecological obligation.

Human Endeavors to Emulate Nature's Flight Transformations: Overcoming any issues
The continuous investigation of flight variations includes a consistent work to overcome any barrier between human-made flight and the style of nature's plans. The continuous journey for biomimicry in avionics endeavors to make airplane that imitate the productivity of birds as well as limit the natural impression. The dance between human development and nature's brightness turns into a cooperative work to accomplish congruity in the skies.

Trip from now on: Difficulties and Open doors
The continuous mission to unwind the secrets of flying artful dance delivers the two difficulties and potential open doors for what's to come. The difficulties incorporate tending to the natural effect of flying, relieving the dangers to transitory species, and exploring the moral contemplations related with arising flight innovations. The amazing open doors lie in saddling the motivation attracted from nature to enhance practical arrangements, ration biodiversity, and hoist how we might interpret the complex dance that unfurl